The Feasts of the LORD

Rehearsals For The End
Ron Cantrell

First edition *Feasts of the Lord* - April 1999
Second printing - July 1999
Third printing - August 2002
Text copyright ©1999 Ron Cantrell
Graphics, design and illustrations by Ron Cantrell
Copyright ©1999 Ron Cantrell

Printing of *Passover, Why We Celebrate* - February 1998
Text copyright ©1998 Ron Cantrell
Printing of *The Fall Feasts of Israel* - September 1998
Text copyright ©1998 Ron Cantrell

Scripture quotations are taken from:
The Holy Bible, New International Version (NIV)
© 1978 by New York International Bible Society,
and the authorized King James Version.

ISBN 0-9704083-1-5

Published and distributed by
Bridges for Peace
PO Box 33145
Tulsa, OK 74153
800-566-1998

PART I - THE SPRING PILGRIMAGE FESTIVALS

PART II - FEASTS OF THE FALL HARVEST

PART III - HANUKKAH AND PURIM

" . . . these are my appointed feasts, the appointed feasts of the LORD, which you are to proclaim as sacred assemblies . . ."

Leviticus 23:2

Why should Christians pay attention to Jewish holidays? I hear this question asked by many people. I wondered for many years myself what the Old Testament had to teach us when all we could ever hope for was in the pages of the New Testament. There are even institutions of higher Christian education that are satisfied to merely touch on the highlights of the Old Testament, thinking that it is filled with stories of the wrath of God.

I like to think of the Old Testament as the First Covenant. The message is not old. The richness of the material transforms the New Testament into a book vibrant with life and meaning. It is like dining at a fancy restaurant as opposed to dropping by a take-out window at the neighborhood fast food stop.

Those holidays that have been labeled "Jewish Holidays" are actually the "Feasts of the Lord." They in fact are "rehearsals" for future prophetic events. Some have been fulfilled and others have not. **Passover** was a rehearsal for deliverance from sin, i.e. Yeshua (Jesus), the sacrificed lamb on the cross. Fifty days after Passover comes **Pentecost**, called *Shavuot* in Hebrew. This festival was a rehearsal for the firstfruits of harvest time. The Holy Spirit descended on this holiday. He, being the down-payment or firstfruit of our redemption, was poured out upon the disciples, as celebrants from all over the world, who had come up to Jerusalem for this pilgrimage festival, looked on.

The Fall Festivals have not yet been fulfilled. **The Feast of Trumpets** or *Rosh Hashana* in Hebrew, symbolizes the call to the final harvest. The New Testament states that we shall all arise at the "last trump," leaving us a mental picture of the biblical Feast of Trumpets which does indeed fall at the end of the yearly festival cycle (I Cor. 15:52). We do indeed live in the end of the earth's history and await the "trump of God," which signals the final harvest.

Other holidays as well serve to instruct us in the depth of God's love for His people, both Jew and Gentile alike. We are a commonwealth of faith and will enjoy the fulfillment of the Feasts of the Lord. Abraham is our corporate father and mentor - a man who walked in obedience to the Lord at every turn, and through Yeshua, we have been adopted as sons of the promises of God.

Part I
The Spring Pilgrimage Festivals

Passover
The Time of Our Liberation

Part I of the book endeavors to relate the richness and history of Passover, one of the biblical Levitical pilgrimage festivals. The book also includes a brief *Haggadah* (the re-telling), the manual of instruction used in Jewish homes as they celebrate the Passover Seder with their families, and indeed, retell the ancient story of liberation from the bondage of slavery in Egypt.

The Haggadah explains how and why Passover is to be observed. *Seder* is a Hebrew word whose root meaning is "to organize." Therefore, the Passover Seder is *the order* in which the festival is celebrated and in which the meal is conducted.

Whether we actually lived in Egypt and personally escaped slavery, or whether we are Jewish or Christian, the remembrance of this important event in the chronology of God's chosen people is meaningful. We benefit from counting ourselves to have escaped the bondage of sin.

To really understand Passover, we must understand the events in Egypt leading up to the Exodus of the Hebrew Israelites. The texture of Egyptian social and religious life has much to do with what followed later in the wilderness.

As this moment of history unfolds, the Israelites have been cut off from their Hebrew forefathers by the passing of some 430 years. All those who knew firsthand what brought the Israelites to Egypt were now dead. We find them dwelling in a land far from their ancestral home, working in the lowly position of servant-class. This servanthood was probably not slavery as we think of it today. The technology of Egypt was not mastered and maintained by a downtrodden slave class. Many of the Hebrews were craftsmen of the highest quality, although in servant-class status. The quality of their craftsmanship was later displayed when the Hebrews Bezalel and Oholiab, filled with the Spirit of the Lord, oversaw the crafting of the Tabernacle in the wilderness.

Unlike the sojourn to Babylon, the Hebrews were not in Egypt as punishment for their wrongdoing. But, if the Israelites were to exit Egypt, how would Egypt operate with the decimation of their working class? These thoughts must have plagued Pharaoh. At the end of this 430 year period, the children of Israel are ripe for deliverance and God is ready to bring them out of Egypt with His mighty hand of deliverance. In this, He purposes to show Egypt that He reigns supreme over the multiple gods of the Egyptian religion. The plagues listed in the book of Exodus stand as an audio-visual renunciation of these gods.

The Gods of Egypt

There will be loud wailing
throughout Egypt-worse than
there has ever been or ever will
be again. But among the
Israelites not a dog will
bark at any man or
animal. Then you will know
that the LORD makes a distinction
between Egypt and Israel.

Exodus 11:6,7

Egypt's Gods Judged

There is a three-fold purpose in God's deliverance plan. First, to bring His people out with His mighty deeds; second, to show Egypt the one true God; and lastly, to forge a nation from the mass of dependent humanity that the chosen people had become.

The plagues leading up to the release of the Hebrews came in waves. Those waves came three plagues at a time. Each group progressed in severity until the final blow. Plague number ten was the most severe of all the plagues, with the Angel of Death smiting the firstborn sons of Egypt. The ensuing drama changed the face of Egypt forever.

Moses was instructed to approach Pharaoh on three successive occasions, as he went in the morning to the waters of the Nile River. Most likely, Pharaoh was accompanied by those who would daily check the level of the Nile in order to set the times of the festivals of the river-god. Some of these plagues were direct proclamations against the multiple gods of the Egyptian pantheon. Others were aimed at how those gods were worshiped.

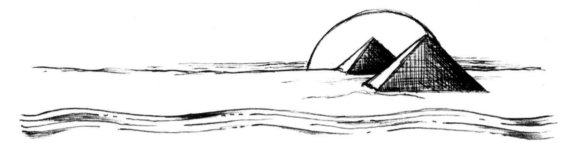

The River

The first plague was against the Nile river itself. The Nile had been deified by the Egyptians as the god Hopi, to whom many hymns of praise can be found amongst their hieroglyphics. The ebb and flow of the river and the overflowing of its banks on a yearly basis, brought life to the Nile River Valley like no other place in the surrounding area. The Egyptians were renowned for their cleanliness and hygienic lifestyles. These plagues were ordained to capture the attention of the populous of Egypt and prepare them to gladly bid good-bye to the Hebrews.

The Frogs

Plague number two was aimed at the deified form of a frog known as Heqt. The goddess Heqt was known to aid women in childbirth. Shlomo Riskin writes a commentary in the Jerusalem Post on the weekly Torah portion (a weekly synagogue reading which systematically works its way through the first five books of Moses in a one year period). Many years ago he wrote about the plague of frogs and the quality of this commentary has never left me. It bears repeating.

Riskin says the eighth chapter of the book of Exodus records, in Hebrew, that only "one frog" came up on the land (Exodus 8:6). This echoes the mass psychosis of anti-semitism in a strange way. One frog comes up and begins to croak loudly. That call goes forth throughout the land, rousing a reaction in other frogs, who then cannot help themselves but that they must also join the bellowing. The riotous frog-call then becomes a platform to which others can successfully attach themselves with total justification.

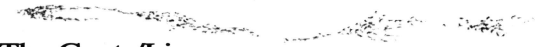

The Gnats/Lice

Gnats or lice, in quantity like the dust of the air, followed the plague of frogs. Desert climate conditions generally disallowed the presence of gnats and small biting insects. Therefore, this must have been a new irritation to the neurotically hygienic Egyptians.

Flies or Beetles

Flies, may be better interpreted from Hebrew, as beetles. *Ha-arob* is the Hebrew term, and is closer to beetle. The beetle, or scarab, was sacred to the Egyptians and regarded as the emblem of the Sun-god Ra. It was sculptured on monuments, painted on tombs, engraved on gems, worn around the neck as an amulet, and honored in ten thousand images.

Death to Livestock

The plague against livestock was one of greater degree than what we have yet seen. An understanding of the importance of livestock in the Egyptian religion is vital.

Edwin M. Yamauchi, in his masterful work, *Persia and the Bible*, gives details on livestock in Egypt. The Egyptians worshiped many animals, but few took such place as the Apis bull. The Egyptian bull-god, Hapi, was regarded as the incarnation of Ptah, the creator god of Memphis. It was held that Ptah inseminated Apis' mother, Isis, with celestial fire. The Apis bull had to exhibit certain characteristics to be considered a representation of the deity.

14

According to the historian, Herodotus (3:28), the marks of the calf called Apis are these: he is black; he has on his forehead a three-cornered white spot; the likeness of an eagle on his back; his tail hairs are double; and there is a knot under the tongue.

The Apis was selected by carefully observed signs, and taken to a special temple where he was pampered all his life. The installation of the Apis was with great ceremony and celebration. In light of this knowledge, the conduct of the Israelites in the wilderness, upon the casting of their golden calf, becomes clearer. They were mimicking conduct that they had become accustomed to in the civil administration of their temporary Egyptian homeland.

The Apis was observed during certain times of the year in a special courtyard in the temple area. His movements were interpreted as oracular signs on a national level. Egypt's future well-being was read in the movements of the Apis.

In 1941, near the temple of Ptah at Memphis, a number of objects associated with the Apis were discovered. These included four alabaster altars, a limestone manger, stands possibly used for an awning to shade the animal, and a large offering table (12 feet by 6 feet) used for washing and mummifying the bull upon its death. The bulls were carefully embalmed and entombed in gigantic sarcophagi (crypts) carved from monolithic blocks of granite, measuring about 10 feet high, 13 feet long, and weighing about 60 to 70 tons. Many of these were uncovered in 1851, some 20 miles southwest of Cairo at Saqqara. They were found in underground galleries about 1,000 feet long. Beside these were numerous bronze statuettes of the bull. It could be that Israelite craftsmen had a hand in creating these likenesses.

The death of the Apis was akin to the death of a Pharaoh. The Apis was considered a god. National mourning struck on the level of hysteria. It has been confirmed archaeologically that the worship of the Apis went back to the First Dynasty, and no doubt had its roots in prehistoric times.

Numbered among the other livestock worshiped by the Egyptians was Mnevis, another bull-god; the cow-god, Hathor; and the ram-god, Khnum.

Festering Boils

This plague followed hard on the heels of the plague upon the livestock. The record states that festering boils broke out on men and on animals throughout the land. Soot from a furnace, a symbol of the toil at brickmaking that the Israelites were forced to do, was thrown into the air. The immediate result was boils on men *and* animals.

Egypt deified many other animals. A sacred animal necropolis was discovered in the 1960s. Terraces, temples, ramps, and galleries had been dedicated to the gods. Four million mummified ibises, five hundred baboons (both sacred to Thoth), five hundred thousand hawks (representations of the god Horus), and a score of cows, representing Isis, the mother of the Apis bull, were found. This plague was attacking Egypt's hoard of sacred animals.

The Hailstorm

Job 38 asks: "*Have you entered into the treasuries of the snow, or seen the storehouses of the hail, which I have reserved for times of trouble . . .?*" This incredible tidbit of scriptural information leads to the next plague. The worst hailstorm to ever hit Egypt took place. A winter plague would take Egypt by surprise and destroy crops vital to the well-being of the population during the following year. Transportation of crops in those days was rare. If you lost the crops you were planning to harvest the following spring and summer, there was no other food supply. It was devastating. The only place the hailstorm did not touch was the land of Goshen, where the Israelites lived.

The Plague of Locusts

One of the most powerful symbols of divine judgement following the hail storm was the plague of locusts. The hail most likely arrived in January and February, as the Bible account tells us that the flax and barley were in bloom, which were both winter crops. The locusts most likely followed in the spring, when the fruit was on the trees. The biblical account tells us that the locust plague was the worst Egypt had ever seen and that there would never be another like it. The land was black with crop-stripping grasshoppers. Harvest time was generally a time of great celebration acknowledging that the gods had provided for your needs. There was no one to whom Egypt could turn when their crops failed on such a catastrophic level.

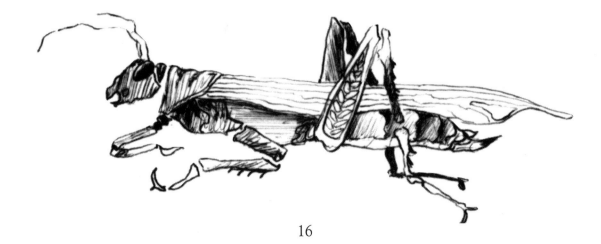

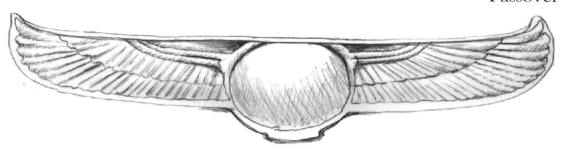

Darkness and the Sun-God Ra

The plague of darkness, so dark it could be felt, was an obvious insult to the sun-god, Ra. Winged-disc of gold with arms descending in benevolent giving - symbol of all that was good in a sun-drenched land. This darkness may have been a dust storm riding the tail winds of the strong wind that blew the locusts into Egypt. Wind storms of frightening proportions are caused by a well known phenomena called a "hamsin." This is a hot violent desert wind that carries tons of dust across the open desert in great billowing clouds almost gray-green in color. Dust fills your mouth, eyes, water pots, and food. There is no way to keep it out. Even today, with modern windows closed and sealed you can still taste the dust of a hamsin. The land of Goshen may have lain far enough north to miss the plague that struck the rest of Egypt.

Somewhat like a stage production, darkness falls in order to spotlight the final act. Pharaoh was coming to the end of his patience and God was coming to the end of His order of attacks against the gods of Egypt. Egypt would now change forever and never regain its glory.

The Angel of Death Strikes the Firstborn

By strict instruction from the mouth of God, each Israelite family, on the tenth day of the month, was to take a year-old male lamb into their home. For four days they lived with the lamb, separated from all the other animals. On the fourteenth day of the month at twilight they slaughtered it. Then they were to place the blood of the lamb on the doorposts and the lintel of the door of the dwelling where they were to eat the roasted lamb. They were to eat their meal prepared to rush off.

On that night, God judged the gods of Egypt. All the protection that those gods were supposed to provide was undone. The most important item to any family of that day and age, a firstborn male, would be taken from them. Even the firstborn animals were slain, to show the ineffectual power of Egypt's man-made gods.

It is noteworthy that after this plague, but before the giving of the law at Mt. Sinai, a rite was instituted among the Israelites that was observed throughout the Israelites' history and is still observed to this day. The custom is called, *Pideon HaBen*, meaning the redemption of the firstborn son. In the book of Exodus, it stands as an oral injunction to Moses, but later becomes law in Leviticus. Until the destruction of the Temple this law was carried out. Now it is a ceremonial rite in the synagogue.

In Exodus 13, after the Israelites flee Egypt, God tells Moses to consecrate to Him the first-born male of both man and animal. In obedience to this law, Jesus, Mary's firstborn son, was taken by Joseph and Mary to be consecrated at the Temple. Simeon, a faithful servant of the Temple, had awaited patiently God's promise of salvation. By the unction of the Spirit of the Lord, Simeon proclaimed Jesus to be the Messiah. A matter should be established by the mouth of at least two witnesses. Therefore, Luke records that the prophetess Anna added to Simeon's proclamation, assuring that He was the fulfillment of all who were looking forward to the redemption of God's people.

The last plague, the Angel of Death, stands as a symbolic foreshadowing of God's future redemption, not only of the Jewish people, but of all the world. The other plagues were attacks against Egyptian gods, but this plague was an attack into the dark territory of Satan himself. The Angel of Death was not an Egyptian god. The belief in local gods was common not only in Egypt but in all surrounding nations. God's offensive attack here, therefore, struck below the surface of religion, a false front to the more universal reality of God's enemy and his dark plans.

Let My People Go!

"Let my people go that they may worship me." This command was given to Pharoah 9 times in the book of Exodus. God explains His two-fold purpose in this command. Let My people go is followed by, *". . . that they may worship Me."* God sought to teach the Israelites not only to be a nation but to renew their worship thereby testifying to the world the character of the God of Israel.

The Exodus ushered the children of Israel into the wilderness, the crucible, used by God to mold a nation. To turn a mass of dependent people into a nation living independently took 40 years. We have usually blamed the Israelites for grumbling and complaining and turning their backs on God in the wilderness, but God's patience with them could not be better portrayed than in the story of Balaam, the "rent-a-prophet."

18

Numbers chapter 23 recounts Balaam's "oracles-for-hire" against Israel. The oracles were diametrically opposed to King Balak's desires. The contents of those proclamations by Balaam reveal God's heart about His people coming out of the desert. Balaam asks, *"How can I curse those whom God has not cursed?"* He continues in the second oracle to pronounce that, *"He (God) has not looked on Jacob's offenses or on the wrongs found in Israel. The Lord their God is with them, the shout of a King is among them."* Balaam rises to a pinnacle of prophecy in the fourth oracle about Jacob. *"A star will come out of Jacob, a scepter will rise out of Israel,"* he prophesies, *"A ruler will come out of Jacob . . ."*

It would appear as if God overlooked Israel's sins in the wilderness. God's correction of His people was between Him and them, not given to the authority of a Gentile prophet. On the contrary, God looked at the potential of His people, even though their time of testing was not over. He preferred to manifest His mercy before outsiders, and judge sin within the camp.

We have also viewed the wilderness as a symbol of spiritual dryness. Actually, all outside stimuli removed, the wilderness was a place to "*see* God" very clearly. Pillar of fire by night, and a cloud to lead by day. Realistically, Egypt was the place of spiritual dryness. It was a place where your concentration was robbed by too much to do; too much effort making ends meet; too many decisions to make regarding everyday life. The wilderness provided just the right environment for God to train the children of Abraham, Isaac, and Jacob, to be a nation whose only God was the Lord.

The fact is that the children of Israel had changed while in Egypt. 430 years equals roughly 6 or 7 generations. We have no solid proof that they sacrificed any longer. It seems that they had no close relationship with God. When Moses arrived they asked him *who* sent him. The time period of the Exodus is somewhere in the XVIII Dynasty of the Egyptian empire. According to most Bible scholars, the date of the exit of the Hebrews is somewhere between 1450 BC to 1200 BC. The only solid record of the event is in the pages of the Bible.

Because there is no extrabiblical account of the Exodus, some scholars have come to the conclusion that it is a myth. The culture of the Egyptians though, bears their fingerprints during the XVIII Dynasty. The first fingerprint is Egypt's Pharoah Amenhotep who led a movement pressing the Egyptians to adopt the worship of one god. Amenhotep later changed his own name to Akenaten meaning "servant of the one god." It seems that perhaps the theology of the Hebrews had influenced him.

The second fingerprint involves one of Egypt's gods that we did not mention in the previous list of gods. Her name is Sakmet. The name Sakmet means "The Powerful One." Sakmet was a female figure with the head of a lion wearing a large shoulder-length braided wig. The legendary story of Sakmet says that since the Egyptians rebelled against the authority of the sun god Ra, that he would strike a blow at their population and use Sakmet to wade in their blood. The plan is later reneged upon by Ra. The sun god assuages Sakmet's stirred up anger by giving her blood colored beer which calms her. It seems possible that the Egyptians losing the heir to the throne of Pharoah with the death of the firstborn, and then losing the reigning Pharoah who drowned in the Red Sea chasing the Hebrews, could not come to grips with the truth of what they had witnessed. They may have created the legend of the "anger" of Sakmet to explain away the truth of God's intervention on behalf of the Hebrews for their future generations.

God had a purpose for Pharaoh's existence. According to the New Testament book of Romans the usefulness of Egypt's god king was for the sake of the whole world.

> *For the Scripture says to Pharaoh, "I raised you up for this very purpose, that I might display my power in you and that my name might be proclaimed in all the earth."*
>
> Romans 9:17

One final thought provoking point struck me when reading the Hebrew account of the Exodus. An interesting word appears in the Scripture:

> *Moses saw that the people were running wild and that Aaron had let them get out of control and so become a laughing stock to their enemies. So he stood at the entrance to the camp and said, "Whoever is for the LORD, come to me." and all the Levites rallied to him.*
>
> Exodus 32:25

"Running wild," and "out of control" is *paruah*, and is the same root word as in Prov 29:18 translated "perish."

> *Where there is no vision, the people perish.*
>
> Proverbs 29:18

Actually it means to "throw off restraint" or "go backward" as if you were returning to a time that was more comfortable to you. The ironic thing is that it sounds much like the Hebrew word for *Pharaoh.* It seems you can take the Israelites out of Egypt but it is hard to take Egypt (the "Pharoah wildness") out of the Israelites.

In all this, the Scripture is certainly true, God's name has been proclaimed in all the earth, faithfully, from year to year through the celebration of the Passover by Jewish people. Annually the story is recounted, inseparably linked to the name of the Pharoah of Egypt. The vivid mental pictures in the retelling of the story that it creates in the minds of children is handed down faithfully each year by parents as awed by the account as are the children.

The Meal
of Remembrance

The Memorial

"This is a day you are to commemorate; for the generations to come you shall celebrate it as a festival to the Lord - a lasting ordinance. For seven days you are to eat bread made without yeast" (Exodus 12:14). The most widely accepted date for the Exodus from Egypt is somewhere between 1290 and 1446 B.C.

The Feast of Passover

On the Jewish calendar month of Nisan, on the fourteenth day of that month, the Jewish people celebrate a memorial holiday by eating a meal together called the Passover Seder. Themes of the holy day are: deliverance; spiritual maturity; and a move toward a more intimate relationship with God. The celebration of this meal is with the hope that we will remember where we came from and give praise for God's deliverance.

Spring cleaning may have its origins in the customs of the Jewish people during the week before Passover. The biblical injunction is that no yeast is to be found in your house. Yeast or leaven is an often used symbol for sin in the pages of the Bible. Jewish homes are cleaned from top to bottom in a search to rid one's home of all leavening. Once the house has been rid of all traces of leavening, the Passover Seder can begin.

✡✡ The Haggadah ✡✡

The night of Passover is orchestrated by the leader, whether it be the father of the family or a pre-appointed leader, and is led using a book called the Haggadah. Most editions of the Haggadah will have the order of the Seder complete with the traditional Hebrew prayers and songs of celebration. There are many versions of the Haggadah and they may differ one from another, but all Haggadot (plural of Haggadah) include the basic traditional points.

The express purpose of the Seder, (Hebrew word meaning, 'the order of') is to recount (or retell, *le haggid* in Hebrew) the story of the escape from the bondage of Egypt. The story must be kept as a memorial with which to teach the succeeding generations of how God, "with a mighty hand," delivered the children of Israel from the enslavement of Pharaoh.

An Overview of the Seder

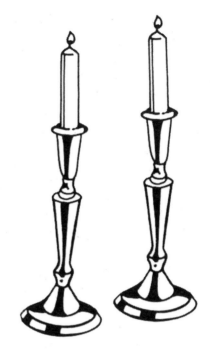

Lighting of the festival candles

Explanation of the Seder Plate

KADESH - Sanctification

URCHATZ - Purification

KARPAS - Greens dipped

YACHATZ - Afikomen hidden

MAGGEED - Unleavened bread

FARAKASHA - Four questions asked

THE TEN PLAGUES - Drops of juice on plate

DAYEINU - It would have been enough

MAROR - Bitter herbs

TZAFUNE - Communion

ELIYAHU - Elijah the prophet welcomed

The Seder Plate

A large round plate is the center piece of the Seder table. On the plate are visual instruction tools with which to tell the story of the first Passover.

There are four cups of wine, or grape juice, to be consumed during the course of the Seder meal. These can be partaken of from one cup to save space and having to place so many cups on one table. The cups are very meaningful and each have a name. They are:

1. The Cup of Sanctification
2. The Cup of Plagues
3. The Cup of Redemption
4. The Cup of Praise
5. The Cup of Elijah - Not partaken of until Messiah comes

The Plate Items Are:

I. Karpas: A vegetable. Parsley is normally used as it is green symbolizing spring, life, and vitality. It is dipped in salt water near the beginning of the Seder to ymbolize the safe passage through the Red Sea on the way to freedom.

II. Haroset: A mixture of apples, nuts, wine and spices (nutmeg, a touch of cloves, and cinnamon). This mixture is made to resemble the mortar, (brown, sticky and mushy) used by the Egyptian slaves to put together their hand-made bricks.

III. Maror: Bitter herbs are to remind us of the "bitterness of slavery." This is symbolic of the early Israelites' slavery in Egypt and our own slavery to sin before our deliverance. Usually horseradish is used as the bitter herb. It must bring tears to our eyes!

IV. Beitzah: A roasted egg is a symbol of the festival sacrifice that would have been offered by each Jewish person going up to the Temple in Jerusalem. The egg should be baked in the oven, still in its shell, and basted with very strong tea to give a nice, roasted coloring.

V. Zeroa: A roasted bone, commonly a shank bone, that has been roasted over the fire. An alternative to a shank bone is a chicken wing bone or even a broiled beet.

VI. Matzot: These are the flat, unleavened bread substitutes. They look like very large crackers and can be bought in almost any supermarket in the spring. Three of these are placed together, one on top of the other, and then covered with a white napkin.

Other items to have on the table

Salt Water: We dip the karpas (green vegetable) into the salt water, a symbol of the passage through the salty Red Sea as well as the tears of slavery.

Reclining: In ancient times, reclining at a meal was a symbol of freedom. Slaves ate either standing up or squatting down, never in a comfortable position. A pillow placed on your chair is traditionally the symbol of reclining during the Passover Seder today.

Elijah's Cup: According to legend, Elijah may come to visit the home on Passover to announce the arrival of the Messiah. A large ornate cup has been traditionally set somewhere on the table with the expectation that we may, indeed, be living in the time of the Messiah's coming and that Elijah could come and join our Seder dinner easily.

Outline of the Dinner

I. Lighting the candles: In Jewish homes, the lighting of the holiday candles separates the sacred from the mundane. This holiday is set apart from the normal days of the year, like the Sabbath day of rest is separated from the week's cares. The woman of the house lights the candles as she is seen as the one who brings light and warmth to the home.

(Light the candles and say:)

Blessed art thou, O Lord our God, King of the universe
who has commanded us to light the holiday candles.

Baruch ata Adonai, Eloheinu Melech Ha-olam,
Asher kidshanu b'mitzvotav, v'tzivanu
l'hadlik ner shel yom tov.

בָּרוּךְ אַתָּה יי אֱלֹהֵינוּ מֶלֶךְ הָעוֹלָם
אֲשֶׁר קִדְּשָׁנוּ בְּמִצְוֹתָיו וְצִוָּנוּ
לְהַדְלִיק נֵר שֶׁל יוֹם טוֹב.

II. Kadesh: The meal is set aside to the purposes of God by praying over the first cup of
wine or grape juice and sanctifying the evening. The prayer is: "Blessed art Thou O
Lord our God, King of the Universe, who has kept us alive and preserved us and enabled
us to reach this season." Everyone then partakes of the first cup of wine or grape juice.
The prayer in Hebrew is as follows:

Baruch ata Adonai, Eloheinu
Melech HaOlam, Asher b'char
banu m'kol am, V'rom-me-manu
m'kol lashon, v'kid-sha-nu b'mitz-
vo-tav. V'te-ten-lanu Adonai Eloheinu b'a-ha-va moadeem l'sim-cha
haggim u'zmanim l'sasson et yom
hag ha-matzot ha-zeh.
Z'man cheruteinu meek-rey kodesh
zacher letziat Mitzraiim. Keyvanu

סָבְרִי מָרָנָן וְרַבָּנָן וְרַבּוֹתַי׃

בָּרוּךְ אַתָּה יְיָ אֱלֹהֵינוּ מֶלֶךְ
הָעוֹלָם בּוֹרֵא פְּרִי הַגָּפֶן׃

בָּרוּךְ אַתָּה יְיָ אֱלֹהֵינוּ מֶלֶךְ
הָעוֹלָם אֲשֶׁר בָּחַר־בָּנוּ מִכָּל־
עָם וְרוֹמְמָנוּ מִכָּל־לָשׁוֹן וְקִדְּשָׁנוּ
בְּמִצְוֹתָיו. וַתִּתֶּן־לָנוּ יְיָ אֱלֹהֵינוּ
בְּאַהֲבָה (שַׁבָּתוֹת לִמְנוּחָה וּ) מוֹעֲדִים

לְשִׂמְחָה חַגִּים וּזְמַנִּים לְשָׂשׂוֹן
אֶת־יוֹם (הַשַּׁבָּת הַזֶּה וְאֶת־יוֹם) חַג
הַמַּצּוֹת הַזֶּה. זְמַן חֵרוּתֵנוּ (בְּאַהֲבָה)
מִקְרָא קֹדֶשׁ זֵכֶר לִיצִיאַת מִצְרָיִם.
כִּי בָנוּ בָחַרְתָּ וְאוֹתָנוּ קִדַּשְׁתָּ מִכָּל־
הָעַמִּים (וְשַׁבָּת) וּמוֹעֲדֵי קָדְשֶׁךָ
(בְּאַהֲבָה וּבְרָצוֹן) בְּשִׂמְחָה וּבְשָׂשׂוֹן
הִנְחַלְתָּנוּ. בָּרוּךְ אַתָּה יְיָ מְקַדֵּשׁ
(הַשַּׁבָּת וְ) יִשְׂרָאֵל וְהַזְּמַנִּים׃

v'char-ta v'otanu kedashta m'kol ha-amim u'mo-a-day kad-sha-cha b'sim-cha u'va-sasson hin-chal-tanu.
Baruch ata Adonai m'kadesh Yisrael v'ha-zmaniim.

III. Urchatz: The leader of the Seder, or the father of the family, ceremonially washes his hands
from a pitcher at the table and dries his hands on a towel.

IV. Karpas: We now dip the green vegetable into the salt water and recount the struggles of slavery and how bitter were the tears in Egypt.

Blessed art thou, O Lord Our God
King of the Universe,
Creator of the fruits of the earth.
(The vegetable is eaten.)

בָּרוּךְ אַתָּה יְיָ אֱלֹהֵינוּ מֶלֶךְ
הָעוֹלָם בּוֹרֵא פְּרִי הָאֲדָמָה׃

Baruch ata Adonai Eloheinu melech ha-olam, boreh pre ha-adamah.

25

V. Yachatz: We take the middle matzah cracker on the table, break it in half, cover one of the halves with a white napkin and hide it somewhere. (Make sure that the children do not see you hide this piece of matzah as they will later search for the cracker to redeem it for a monetary reward.) This piece that is set aside is called by the Aramaic name - *afikomen* - meaning dessert. Some sources have indicated that this portion of the meal is redemptive and that the hidden piece of matzah is symbolic of a coming redemption. We are to save the hidden piece until last and must not eat anything after it, so that we leave the Passover Seder with the taste of redemption on our lips.

VI. Maggid: (another form of the Hebrew verb *le-haggid* = meaning, to tell): This is the actual narration of the story of the Exodus. It follows a form as well.

a. *Ho lach-ma ahnya* - This explanation is in Aramaic but can be done in English and accomplish the job of explaining just as well. It says, "This is the bread of affliction that our ancestors ate in Egypt. This year we are slaves, next year we shall be free. Let all who are hungry come and eat. Let all who are in need come and share our Passover meal."

הָא לַחְמָא עַנְיָא דִּי אֲכָלוּ   יֵיתֵי וְיִפְסַח. הָשַׁתָּא הָכָא. לְשָׁנָה

אֲבָהָתָנָא בְּאַרְעָא דְמִצְרָיִם. כָּל־   הַבָּאָה בְּאַרְעָא דְיִשְׂרָאֵל. הָשַׁתָּא

כָּל דִכְפִין יֵיתֵי וְיֵכָל. כָּל־דִּצְרִיךְ   עַבְדֵי. לְשָׁנָה הַבָּאָה בְּנֵי חוֹרִין:

Ho lach-ma-an-ya, d'ach-lu av ho-so-no v'ha-ta-na b'ar-re-ah d'Mitzraiim. Kol v'feen y'tay v'yah-kol. Kol deetz-reech y'tay v'yeef-sach. Ho-sha-to ha-cho. L'sha-na ha-ba-ah d'Yisrael. Ha-sha-ta ov-day. Ha-Sha-na ha-ba-ah b'nai ho-reen.

VII. Farakasha: The four questions

Mah Nishtanah - This section requires a child, or youngest member of the family, to ask four questions of the leader of the Seder. Traditionally it is sung. The questions are:

Why is this night different from all other nights?
1. Why on this night do we eat only matzah?
2. Why on this night do we eat bitter herbs?
3. Why on this night do we dip twice?
4. Why on this night do we recline while we eat?

The Hebrew is:

מָרוֹר: שֶׁבְּכָל־הַלֵּילוֹת אֵין אָנוּ   מַה נִּשְׁתַּנָּה הַלַּיְלָה הַזֶּה מִכָּל־

מַטְבִּילִין אֲפִילוּ פַּעַם אֶחָת.   הַלֵּילוֹת: שֶׁבְּכָל־הַלֵּילוֹת אָנוּ

הַלַּיְלָה הַזֶּה שְׁתֵּי פְעָמִים: שֶׁבְּכָל־   אוֹכְלִין חָמֵץ וּמַצָּה. הַלַּיְלָה הַזֶּה

הַלֵּילוֹת אָנוּ אוֹכְלִין בֵּין יוֹשְׁבִין   כֻּלּוֹ מַצָּה: שֶׁבְּכָל־הַלֵּילוֹת אָנוּ

וּבֵין מְסֻבִּין. הַלַּיְלָה הַזֶּה כֻּלָּנוּ   אוֹכְלִין שְׁאָר יְרָקוֹת הַלַּיְלָה הַזֶּה

מְסֻבִּין:

Mah neesh-ta-na ha-lai-la ha-zeh m'kol ha-lai-lot?
1. She-b'kol ha-lai-lot anu och-leen hametz u-matzah.
   Ha-lai-la ha-zeh ku-loh matzah.
2. She-b'kol ha-lai-lot anu och-leen sh-or y'ra-kot,
   Ha-lai-la ha-zeh maror.
3. She-b'kol ha-lai-lot anu mat-be-leen a-fee-lu pa-am echad,
   Ha-lai-la ha-zeh sh'tay pa-amim.
4. She-b'kol ha-lai-lot anu och-leen bayn yosh-veen u'vain m'su-been,
   Ha-lai-la ha-zeh ku-loh m'su'been.

This is the tune to which the four questions are traditionally sung.

MA NISHTANA

27

Following the four questions comes an explanation by the leader, which actually does not answer the four questions specifically, but recounts the history of the Exodus from Egypt. The elements are simple and expounding upon them dramatically is encouraged. (Exodus 4:18 to 13:22 recounts the story for a condensed reading as an alternative).

VIII. Ten Plagues: This is the second cup of wine or grape juice. As the leader of the group pronounces the names of all the plagues of Egypt, each person sticks his finger in his cup of wine and places a drop on his plate, representing each plague. The plagues, listed first in Hebrew, then in English, are:

Dam - Water changed to Blood
Tzfardeyah - Frogs
Kinim - Lice/Gnats
Arov - Flies/Beetles
Dever - Blight
Sh'hin - Boils
Barad - Hail
Arbeh - Locusts
Hoshech - Darkness
Makat B'horot - Slaying of the firstborn.

At this point, a traditional song called "*Dayeinu*" is sung, which means, "It Would Have Been Enough for Us." This song says that if God had just taken us out of Egypt, it would have been enough, but look at what all else He has done for us. (This is followed by reciting Psalms 113 and 114 all together. These two Psalms are the beginning of the Great Hallel, which means "praise." After the meal, which is yet to come, the continuation of the Hallel is sung with great gusto. Far into the night, thanks to God for all He has done continues, with singing, dancing and great celebration.)

The second cup of wine is now raised again and the blessing is said.
With the second cup of wine we recall the second promise of liberation:
As it is written: ". . . I will deliver you from their bondage . . . " (Exodus 6:6).

Blessed art thou, O Lord our God, King of the Universe, who createst the fruit of the vine.

בָּרוּךְ אַתָּה יְיָ אֱלֹהֵינוּ מֶלֶךְ הָעוֹלָם, בּוֹרֵא פְּרִי הַגָּפֶן:

Baruch ata Adonai Eloheinu melech ha-olam, boreh pre ha-gafen.

Now all partake of the second cup together.

28

DAYEINU

I - lu ho - tzi ho - tzi - a - nu, ho - tzi - a - nu mi - mitz - ra - yim,

ho - tzi - a - nu mi - mitz - ra - yim da - yei - nu.

(Chorus) Da - da - yei - nu,____ da - da - yei - nu,____ da - da - yei - nu, da -

yei - nu da - yei - nu da - yei - nu. yei - nu da - yei - nu.

2. I-lu na-tan, na-tan la-nu, na-tan la-nu et ha-sha-bat, na-tan la-nu
et ha-sha-bat, dayeinu. (Chorus).

3. I-lu na-tan, na-tan la-nu, na-tan la-nu et ha-to-rah, na-tan la-nu et
ha-to-rah, dayeinu. (Chorus.)

4. I-lu na-tan, na-tan la-nu, na-tan la-nu et Ye-shua, na-tan la-nu
et Ye-shua, dayeinu. (Chorus).

The Great Hallel

Psalm 113

Praise the LORD! Praise, O servants of the Lord. Praise the name of the LORD! Blessed be the name of the LORD from this time forth and forever more! From the rising of the sun to the going down, the LORD's name is to be praised.

The LORD is high above all nations, His glory above the heavens. Who is like the LORD our God? Who dwells on high, Who humbles Himself to behold the things that are in the heavens and in the earth?

He raises the poor out of the dust, and lifts the needy out of the ash heap, that He may seat him with princes - with the princes of His people. He grants the barrren woman a home, like a joyful mother of children.

Praise the Lord!

Psalm 114:

When Israel went out of Egypt, the house of Jacob from a people of strange language, Judah became His sanctuary, and Israel His dominion.

The sea saw it and fled; Jordan turned back. The mountains skipped like rams. The little hills like lambs. What ails you, O sea, that you fled? O Jordan, that you turned back? O mountains, that you skipped like rams: O little hills, like lambs.

Tremble, O earth, at the presence of the LORD. At the presence of the God of Jacob, Who turned the rock into a pool of water, The flint into a fountain of waters.

IX. Maror: Now the leader breaks off pieces of the upper and middle matzah and distributes a piece to everyone. Everyone then dips his matzah into the *maror* (horseradish) and eats together. Traditionally, enough must be eaten to bring tears to the eyes. This is to remind us of how bitter slavery was. You can then follow quickly with the *haroset* (the apple, nut, cinnamon mixture), to remember how slavery was sweetened by the redemption provided by God.

Blessed art thou, O Lord Our God, King of the Universe, who hast sanctified us with thy commandments, and commanded us to eat bitter herbs.

בָּרוּךְ אַתָּה יְיָ אֱלֹהֵינוּ מֶלֶךְ
הָעוֹלָם אֲשֶׁר קִדְּשָׁנוּ בְּמִצְוֹתָיו וְצִוָּנוּ
עַל־אֲכִילַת מָרוֹר:

Baruch ata Adonai Eloheinu melech ha-olam, Asher kidshanu
b'mitzvotav v'tzivanu al-achilat maror.

X. The Meal
It is now time to serve the meal and everyone enjoys a delightful feast together.

XI. Tzafune: Communion. After the meal is finished, the leader will let the children know that it is time to search for the afikomen, which has been hidden away and buried. When the afikomen is found, each person at the table needs to contribute together for the monetary reward going to the child who located the afikomen.

The symbolism of this unleavened bread of affliction, which has been hidden away is now brought to the forefront in Luke as Yeshua, with His disciples, prepares to make this meal a memorial of His atoning death.

This piece of matzah is now broken into olive sized pieces and passed out to each person. It will be partaken of with the third cup of wine or grape juice.

XII. The Third Cup - The Cup of Redemption: Luke is the only writer of the Gospels to record for us that the cup that Jesus lifted up and said, *"This is my blood shed for you,"* was the cup *after* the Passover meal. Luke himself was a Gentile and knew that some extra explaining needed to be done for those who would not know the order of a Passover meal. With this cup, Jesus took the bread, broke it and instituted the Lord's supper there at His last meal with His disciples. He added that He would not drink of the fruit of the vine again until He drinks together with His disciples in the Kingdom of Heaven.

Blessed art thou, O Lord our God, King of the Universe, who createst the fruit of the vine.

בָּרוּךְ אַתָּה יְיָ אֱלֹהֵינוּ מֶלֶךְ
הָעוֹלָם, בּוֹרֵא פְּרִי הַגָּפֶן:

Baruch ata Adonai Eloheinu melech ha-olam, boreh pre ha-gafen.

XIII. The Fourth Cup - The Cup of Praise

The desire to celebrate this Feast in Jerusalem has been the prayer of the Jewish people for 2,000 years of their dispersion. Each person now proclaims to someone else at the table, "Next year in Jerusalem."

All lift the cup reciting together:

Blessed art Thou, O Lord our God, King of the universe, Who createst the fruit of the vine. (Same as blessing above)

Now ending the Seder, songs are sung from Psalm 115-118 or the section is recited by all. These Psalms lead into the Great Hallel which is Psalm 136.

XIV. Elijah Officially Welcomed

Traditionally, one of the children now proceeds to the door which has been left ajar. The child checks to see if perhaps Elijah has arrived to announce the arrival of the Messiah bringing to a close the Passover Seder.

On that day tell your son,
'I do this because of what
the LORD did for me
when I came out of Egypt.'
. . . For the LORD brought you
out of Egypt with
a mighty hand.

Exodus 13: 8,9

Songs For The Celebration

HÉVÉNU SHALŌM

With joy

Folk tune

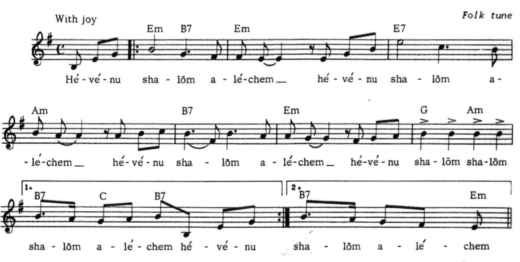

Hé-vé-nu sha-lōm a-lé-chem— hé-vé-nu sha-lōm a-lé-chem— hé-vé-nu sha-lōm a-lé-chem— hé-vé-nu sha-lōm sha-lōm sha-lōm a-lé-chem hé-vé-nu sha-lōm a-lé-chem

Peace unto you!

הֲבֵאנוּ שָׁלוֹם עֲלֵיכֶם

33

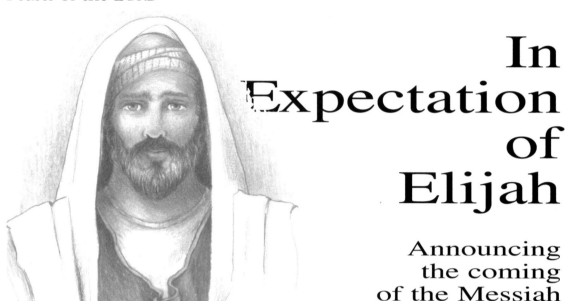

In Expectation of Elijah

Announcing the coming of the Messiah

EILIYAHU HANAVI

Ei - li - ya - hu ha - na - vi, ei - li - ya - hu ha - tish - bi,

Fine

ei - li - ya - hu, ei - li - ya - hu, ei - li - ya - hu ha - gi - la - di.

Bim - hei - ra v' - ya - mei - nu, ya - vo ei - lei - nu

Da capo al Fine

im ma - shi - aḥ ben da - vid, im ma - shi - aḥ ben da - vid.

ARTSA ALINU

Folk tune

Ar-tsa a-li-nu ar-tsa a-li-nu ar-tsa a-li-nu

k'var cha-rash-nu v'-gam za-ra-nu k'var cha-rash-nu v'-gam za-ra-nu

a-val ōd lō ka-tsar-nu a-val ōd lō ka-tsar-nu

We have come to our beloved land. We have plowed and planted but we have not yet harvested our crop.

אַרְצָה עָלִינוּ
כְּבָר חָרַשְׁנוּ וְגַם זָרַעְנוּ
אֲבָל עוֹד לֹא קַצַּרְנוּ

HINÉ MA TŌV

Psalm 133:1
Round I

Folk song

Hi-né ma tov u-ma na-im she-vet a-chim gam yachad

hi-né ma tov u-ma na-im

she-vet a-chim she-vet a-chim gam yachad

Behold how good and pleasant it is for brothers to dwell together in unity.

הִנֵּה מַה טּוֹב וּמַה נָּעִים
שֶׁבֶת אַחִים גַּם יָחַד

35

Avadim Hayinu

S. Postolsky

A-va-dim ha-yi - nu, ha-yi-nu a-tah b'-nei ḥo-rin, — b'-

nei ḥo - rin. A-va-dim_____ ha-yi-nu, a-tah a-tah b'-nei ḥo-rin.__

A-va-dim ___ ha-yi-nu, a-tah a-tah b'-nei ḥo-rin, b'-nei ḥo-rin.

We were slaves – Now we are free men

Ani Ma-amin

אֲנִי מַאֲמִין

הַמִּלִים: רַמְבַּ"ם — הַמַּנְגִּינָה: עֲמָמִית

Ani mamin (3)	אֲנִי מַאֲמִין (3)
Beemuna shleima	בֶּאֱמוּנָה שְׁלֵמָה,
Beviyat haMashiyach (2) } 2	2 { בְּבִיאַת הַמָּשִׁיחַ (2)
Ani mamin . . .	אֲנִי מַאֲמִין . . . .
Veaf ai pi sheyitmameya } 2	2 { וְאַף עַל פִּי שֶׁיִּתְמַהְמֵהַּ,
Im kol ze ani maamin . . .	עִם כָּל זֶה אֲנִי מַאֲמִין . . .

I believe with perfect faith in the coming of the Messiah

36

Mayim Mayim

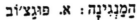

Ushavtem mayim besason	וּשְׁאַבְתֶּם מַיִם בְּשָׂשׂוֹן
Mimayney hayeshua.	מִמַּעַיְנֵי הַיְשׁוּעָה.
Mayim (4) Ho mayim besason (2)	(2) מַיִם (4) הוֹי, מַיִם בְּשָׂשׂוֹן
Ha, ha, ha, ha	,הַ,הַ,הַ,הַ
Mayim (6) besason	מַיִם (6) בְּשָׂשׂוֹן
Mayim (6)	(6) מַיִם
Mayim (3) besason (2)	(2) .מַיִם (3) בְּשָׂשׂוֹן

Isaiah 12:3

37

Hiney Mah Tov

Psalm 133:1

Traditional

Hin · ey mah tov u ·
hold, how good and

mah na im, shev et a chim gam yach - ad Hin ·
pleas - ant it is for breth ren to dwell to · geth · er. Be ·

ey mah tov u · · mah na im, shev et a chim gam
hold, how good and — pleas - ant it is for breth ren to dwell to ·

yach - ad. Hin · ey mah tov, hin · ey mah tov. La la
geth - er In u - ni - ity, to dwell in u - ni - ity, La la

la, la la la la la la la, Hin · ey mah tov, hin · ey mah
la, la la la la la la la, In u - ni - ity, to dwell in u - ni

tov. La la la, la la la la la la la, Be ·
ity, La la la, la la la la la la la, la,

Yeshua Celebrates Passover

Passover in Yeshua's Time

As an added bonus to what we have already covered on Passover, Dr. Jim Fleming, founder of Biblical Resources and the Scripture Garden in Jerusalem, provides some facts about a first century biblical meal that sheds light on Jesus' time with His disciples on that night.

Jerusalem was a small city whose population swelled to probably five times its size on the three pilgrimage festivals. Pilgrimage festivals were those in which all of Israel had to come up to Jerusalem to appear before the Lord. They were Passover, Pentecost, and Sukkot.

Where would an itinerant rabbi and his twelve disciples find a place "prepared" for them to partake of Passover together in a city bustling with activity for the holidays? There are clues in the story that help us reconstruct the events of that night.

Reading in Luke's Gospel, Jesus sent His disciples to find a man carrying a water pot. Male and female jobs were more gender delineated in Jesus' time period and the carrying of water for household use was generally done by women. Jesus told them when they found the man, to follow him to a house where they were to tell the owner, *"The Teacher asks: Where is the guest room where I may eat the Passover with My disciples?"* (Luke 22:7-12)

Two important pieces of information present themselves to us in the account. A man with a water jar suggests to us that the man may have been of the Essene community that lived on the shores of the Dead Sea. Few women were allowed into the Essene community, as celibacy was strictly followed. Therefore, most of the community were men and had to do both men's and women's jobs. During pilgrimage festivals, the Essene community made use of a small cloistered sector of the city of Jerusalem on the south side, separated from mainstream Judaism.

Another clue is that Jesus told His disciples to tell the owner of the house, "The Teacher" asks for a place to eat the Passover with his disciples. The Dead Sea scrolls tell us that the Essene community awaited "The Teacher," a Messiah-like figure, who would come to lead them in a "revolt of the Sons Of Light" (as they viewed themselves) against the "Sons of Darkness" (as they viewed mainstream Judaism at the time). Jesus used the familiar terms of the Essene community to find a place to be with His disciples on a night of His most intimate bonding with them. This is the night He would symbolically break His own body and shed His own blood, through the cup and the matzah He would share with them. This meal would institute the communion we now share together as believers in Yeshua the Messiah, as we remember His atoning death.

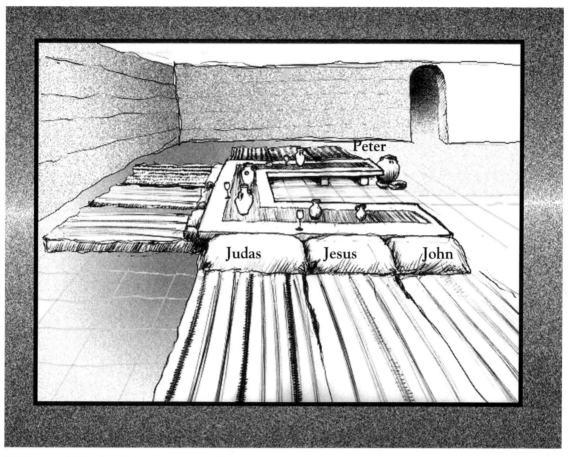

The Triclinium Table

And when the hour had come, He reclined at table with them. "I have earnestly desired to eat this Passover with you."

Luke 22:14,15

The setting of the meal was not Leonardo da Vinci-style. Unlike his painting of the Last Supper where all the diners were seated on one side of a long table laden with puffy, yeasty bread loaves, this table was a reclining table, low to the floor. Its layout, if viewed from above, looked as if you had arranged three long tables in a "U" shape.

The diners lay on their left sides on mats and rested themselves on round pillows that fit snugly close to the table. The center section was left open for servants, who would bring food during the meal. Therefore, the diners' reclining seating arrangements fanned out, radiating from three sides of the table. Though used extensively by the Romans as banqueting arrangements, the method can be traced back in history much further than the Romans.

The seating had its peculiarities as well. Traditions of Kings who had to guard their lives at all costs dictated the seating arrangements. The side of the table closest to the entrance door was reserved for people of least importance. The host, or king, put as much distance as possible between himself and the place where an enemy could enter. Normally four people could fit on one side of a table, the size of the Last Supper table of Jesus and His disciples. The host and guest of honor did not sit at a center table as at banquets today. The host sat in the second seat from the end of the table on the side, furthest from the door. The guest of honor sat just behind him and a good friend sat just in front of the host, also providing some further manner of protection. This was not to say that Jesus was afraid and arranged the table thusly, it was simply the custom of the day.

Jesus' teaching about being invited to a wedding feast will tell us a bit more about the seating arrangements. Jesus taught His disciples never to rush to the seat of honor when invited to a banquet.

> When someone invites you to a wedding feast, do not take the place of honor, for a person more distinguished than you may have been invited. If so, the host who invited both of you will come and say to you, 'Give this man your seat.' Then humiliated, you will have to take the least important place. But when you are invited, take the lowest place, so that when your host comes, he will say to you, 'Friend, move up to a better place.' Then you will be honored in the presence of all your fellow guests. For everyone who exalts himself will be humbled, and he who humbles himself will be exalted.   Luke 14:8-11

Perhaps Peter, seeing John the beloved seated in the seat of the friend closest to Jesus, and Judas seated in the seat of the guest of honor, would have hurriedly made his way to the lowest seat. Perhaps he was hoping all the while that Jesus would say to him, "Come up here" (John 13:22-27).

We know John was seated in front of Jesus. While reclining on his left side, he could simply lean back just a little and be right in Jesus' face to ask him the question about the personage of the betrayer. The Gospels tell us that John leaned on Jesus' breast to ask the question. How much more sense this scene makes, than Leonardo's Last Supper painting. We know Judas had to be in the seat of the guest of honor because Jesus indicated that the betrayer was the one who would dip with him in the dish. Only John and Judas could have been close enough to the communal bowl sitting on the table to dip with Jesus. Meals of this day began with communal dishes, where the diners would "dip" with unleavened bread.

We suspect that Peter was in the last seat, nearest the door, as the account tells us that it was he who asked John to question Jesus about the betrayer. Peter, in that position, was the only one who would have had eye contact with John. Both reclined on their left sides, therefore John's eyes were turned away from everyone except that person in the last seat near the door. Peter may have just picked up an olive pit and tossed it at John to get his attention to instruct him to ask the question.

Passover is rich with meaning for us. Jesus had Passover with His disciples at the most crucial time of His life. Aware of His impending death, one could understand if He had said, "It doesn't matter now, let's just skip all this and go straight to the Garden of Gethsemane." Not so. Jesus had more teaching yet to do, and a last intimate time to share with His beloved followers.

The Marriage Supper of the Lamb may well be the fulfillment of Passover since Jesus said He would not partake of the cup again until He partakes of it with us in heaven.

It is a rewarding experience to share the flavor and color of first century Israel with a biblical meal like our Messiah's Last (Passover) Supper with His disciples.

If you can find a place to participate in a Passover Seder you will find it enriching. If all you are able to do is read and learn of its meaning, you will still discover an educational banquet where we remember the God of our deliverance and salvation, through the atoning blood of the Lamb, Yeshua our Messiah!

From the last day of Passover, we already begin looking forward to the next pilgrimage festival, Shavuot. This festival is also known to the Jewish people as the Feast of Weeks. To the Church it is known as Pentecost.

". . . We hear them
declaring the wonders of God
in our own tongues!"

Amazed
and perplexed,
they asked one another,
"What does this mean?"

Acts 2:11b, 12

SHAVUOT - PENTECOST

A Mighty
Fall Of
Fire

God's Great Ad Campaign

God's Manifest Presence is longed for, sought after, recorded in several exciting instances in the pages of Scripture, and magnetically attractive to us, like nothing else. It seems we can never get enough of reading about it. We long to be where God's presence is - to be refreshed, renewed, enthused in the strictest sense of the Greek word, (*en-theos*, i.e. filled with God).

The terrifying smoking fire on Mount Sinai in the desert, the pillar of fire that led the Hebrews by night, and the mighty fall of God's fire on the Temple Mount some centuries later, recorded in the book of Acts, constitute different, yet linked, events in the chronology of Jewish religious life.

The connecting thread is God's *Shekinah* translated in English as "His Manifest Presence." The symbol of this linking thread is "fire" which empowers His people.

The latter event, from the book of Acts chapter 2, reached out and encompassed new additions to the commonwealth of faith. The group of believers, which later came to be called the Church, were endowed with a baptism of fire on that Feast of Shavuot (Pentecost) 2,000 years ago, standing atop Zion - God's holy mountain. These then dispersed from Jerusalem, taking the message of what they witnessed on the day of Pentecost, testifying to the wonders of God.

Yom HaBikkurim

Shavuot is also known as *Yom Ha-Bikkurim* or the day of "Firstfruits." The fruits of the earliest harvest of the year were presented to God as a thank offering for the larger fall harvest that would follow.

In modern Jewish thought, Shavuot is a memorial of the giving of the Torah, the five books of Moses, at Mount Sinai. The fearful, quaking, burning mountain frightened the people of Israel to the point that they pleaded it never be repeated.

The covenant from Mount Sinai was forged with a people who would from that time forward be providing their sustenance from the fruit of the ground. Therefore, Shavuot is also inseparably linked to the agricultural cycle. It is, as well, one of the three pilgrimage festivals where the faithful came up to Jerusalem for the rituals of the feast.

The Counting of the Omer

> *From the day after the Sabbath, the day that you bring the sheaf of wave offering, you shall keep count until seven full weeks have elapsed: you shall count 50 days until the day after the seventh week, then you shall bring an offering of new grain to the LORD. You shall bring from your settlements two full loaves of bread as a wave-offering . . . . On that same day you shall hold a celebration, it shall be a sacred occasion for you.* Lev 23:15-21

Shavuot is attached to the last day of Passover by a ritual called, "The Counting of the Omer." An omer is a measure of dry grain much like the bushel basket of rural America today. The agricultural theme of the celebration is solidified by such a tie-in. From the Shabbat after Passover, the Israelites were commanded by God to count off seven weeks. At the end of seven weeks, Israelites were to come up to Jerusalem to celebrate Shavuot.

There is no advertisement campaign manager anywhere in the world who could pull off such a perfectly devised media event as the Pentecost that fell just after Jesus ascended into the heavens.

A built-in system engendering anticipation had been in existence since the giving of the book of Leviticus in the wilderness. The weeks between Passover and Shavuot had been initially structured to culminate dynamically at Shavuot. The command to count the "in-between" days engaged

47

each person's mind in an aura of expectancy. We understand that God does nothing by accident. Therefore, this amazing day on Mount Zion, when the fire fell from heaven, had been foreshadowed by the counting of the Omer for centuries.

Pentecost – The Day the Fire Fell

The book of Acts records that on that day, Jewish men from every nation on earth were represented in Jerusalem. They had obeyed the commandment to make the pilgrimage trip up to Jerusalem to worship the Lord at the Temple.

The Jewish world of the first century spread out like the spokes of a wheel from Jerusalem, the hub. Those listed in Acts 2:9-12 make a good study of people groups and where they migrated. Parthians, came from the east, the area southwest of the Caspian Sea where Persia of old existed. The Medes came from just north of that area. Elamites were the people from the ancient kingdom of king Ahasuerus, of the book of Esther, in the southern region. Mesopotamia is the land between the rivers Tigris and Euphrates. This is also ancient Assyria and Babylon. Judea were those from near Jerusalem, and Cappadocia was just south of the Black Sea. Phrygia and Pamphylia are now the Moslem nation of Turkey. Egypt, Lybia, and the Cyrenes were from the northern coast of Africa. Jews and converts to Judaism alike came, and even Rome was represented by a contingency of Jewish people coming up for the pilgrimage festival.

All those present witnessed an amazing event. Described by the first century writers of the Bible as tongues of fire, a visible manifestation of God's presence fell upon the believers. Audible mighty rushing wind shook the house in which they were gathered and a crowd came to see what was happening. This was an echo of previous manifestations of God's presence at which the Jewish world took notice.

God's great deeds were proclaimed in the languages of all those present as the Holy Spirit, the *Ruach HaKodesh* in Hebrew, descended upon the disciples of Yeshua.

Jerusalem did not totally reject Yeshua, the Jewish

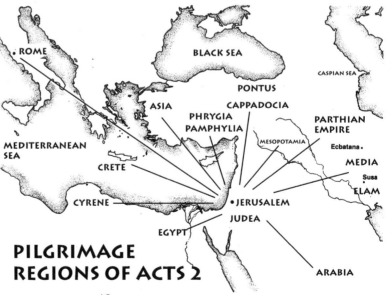

PILGRIMAGE REGIONS OF ACTS 2

Messiah. In a city with a population of 100,000, (though it may have swelled to four times that size on the pilgrimage festivals), 5,000 people came to belief in just a few days time. Even in our day that would make front page news headlines. CNN would even cover it. This puts a stopper in the mouth of anti-Semites who like to repeat the old lie that all the Jews rejected their Messiah and crucified Him. We all share responsibility for Jesus' crucifixion as He gave His life for the sins of the whole world. It is amazing to also realize that all the believers were Jewish until Gentiles came to faith as recorded after chapter 15 of the New Testament book of Acts.

The Book of Ruth

The book of Ruth is read on Shavuot in the synagogue reading cycle. Two themes pervade Shavuot: harvest and revelation. The revelation of the Torah of Moses and a harvest theme could not be married better anywhere else than what we see in the book of Ruth.

The harvest setting of the book of Ruth serves as a perfect backdrop to the unwinding of an important story. Harvesting grain in the ancient Middle East was done in stages. Barley came first, around April, and wheat ripened a few weeks later. In itself, the harvesting process is a treasure store of lessons for us.

A threshing floor of the first century was simple but distinctive. The most important physical prerequisite for a threshing floor was a large slab of exposed bedrock on a hill where the wind could be utilized. Around the perimeter of the slab of bedrock the owner would build a low circular stone wall with several openings for entering the area.

Ruth

Few people owned their own threshing floor. The threshing floor was usually rented from someone fortunate enough to have all the elements that went into making a good threshing area. It seems from the story in the book of Ruth that Boaz must have been the owner of a good threshing floor.

The entire family would come to the threshing floor at harvest time with all their harvested grain. A time schedule would be drawn up for the many families who would need to utilize the threshing area and threshing would begin. Each family came perfectly prepared to begin and finish their job of preparing the grain harvest that would see them

49

through to the next harvest. One could not run out to the supermarket if you ran short of grain during the year.

From the first light of the rising sun, to the last rays of daylight, families would be busy threshing their grain. It is easy to see why the Bible specified that the ox that would be allowed to eat freely of the grain and was not to be muzzled. *"Do not muzzle an ox while it is treading out the grain"* (Deut. 25:4). There were no breaks to be taken in a tight threshing schedule with other families waiting in turn behind you. The ox probably worked from daybreak until dusk.

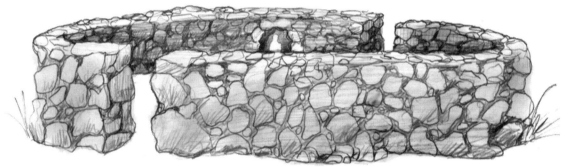

A threshing floor with idol niche

Idolatry

It is important to mention here Israel's fall away from God. Israel often looked around her to see what others were doing and how they functioned in day to day life. The generation that came out of Egypt had never been a nation on their own. They had no resources to draw from about how to accomplish the formidable task of becoming a nation.

When they looked and saw that the Caananites placed small idols in niches in their threshing floor walls to ensure a good harvest, they likewise followed suit. It wasn't that they were throwing out their faith in God. It was more subtle than that. Fear entered into their hearts knowing that if you didn't have enough grain to see you through to the next harvest, you could die. It seemed to make sense to them that a little goddess wouldn't hurt and at best would ensure a good harvest. They still worshiped the God of Israel, but this is one of the reasons God continually called His people to put away their idols and return to him with their whole hearts.

We see then that idolatry is not so much about allowing something that you love, and that captures your attention, to come between you and God. Instead, it is rooted in fear. It is the fear that God can not provide for your needs. Lack of trust minimizes God's power in our lives. Our job of magnifying God to those around us is derailed by this lack of faith which is at the root of idolatry.

Revelation of the Law

How does "revelation" tie in? This part of the book is important for us as Gentiles. We see a theme emerge that is perhaps more familiar to us than to modern day Jewish people. A Gentile woman, Ruth, made a surprising decision to follow her mother-in-law Naomi, into a foreign land, and to accept a God foreign to her background and upbringing. This echoes the acceptance of the Israelites in the wilderness when Moses presented them with the Torah given on the mountain. There had to be a willingness to obey and accept the new revelation that was handed down.

The Exodus led to the desert, the desert led to Mount Sinai, the mountain led to the giving of the Law. The fact that the Israelites accepted God's Law at Sinai eventually led to the coming of the Spirit in power. Otherwise, there would have been no Jerusalem, no Temple Mount, no Jewish nation from which the Messiah would come to fulfill the law.

According to Jewish tradition, King David was born and died on Shavuot. The book of Ruth ends with the genealogy of King David. There is no appointed reading in the synagogue cycle from the book of Ruth. The fact that it is read at Shavuot means that a sector of the Scriptures is being used that is not normally read in the synagogue. That section is called *Ketuvim.* The Jewish Bible is divided into three sections; the Torah, the Prophets, and the other writings known in Hebrew as *Ketuvim.* Each of the beginning letters of the three sections, "T" for *Torah,* "N" for *Neviim* (the Hebrew word for prophets) and "K" for *Ketuvim,* (Hebrew for Scriptures) make up the term that Jewish people use for their Bible, **TeNaK**, spelled and pronounced *Tenach.*

The fact that all the sectors of the Tenach, (Old Testament) are being used during this festival is important to the Jewish people because the totality of the Scriptures is being utilized.

The Fire of God

Back, for a moment, to the Temple Mount on that wonderful day when the "fire of God" fell. This heavenly advertising campaign was perfectly orchestrated. A dynamic lead-in to the event like the "Counting of the Omer" lent an air of expectation. The stage was set for the event that followed. The Holy Spirit came upon the gathered disciples, and men from the four corners of the earth heard of His great deeds in their own languages.

The visible "tongues of fire" echoed in the minds of those present the previous instances where God met His children in a display of power, and authority, often accompanied with fire.

This demonstration of God's Presence sealed the kick-off of a new era within the Jewish religious community. The "believers," as they were first called, were now empowered to carry out the mandate that they had been given. Those who had come up to Jerusalem from the far-reaches of the earth naturally went home with stories to tell about what they had seen and heard. The stage was then set for the harvest which the Shavuot holiday symbolized.

This fire of God purified the disciples of Yeshua, set them apart and endowed them with the mighty power and authority of the Ruach Ha-Kodesh, the Holy Spirit.

Modern Day Traditions

Shavuot today is celebrated by bringing a variety of harvest fruits and stalks of grain with which to decorate the congregation's meeting place. Children are dressed in white with garlands of flowers in their hair. Many schools and *kibbutzim* (agricultural communities) in Israel have a special day set aside for children's presentations with traditional songs of the holiday and specially prepared foods that reflect the first fruits of the season.

It is traditional in some Jewish circles to stay up all night reading the first five books of Moses. Another tradition along that same line is to read all the Psalms aloud to commemorate King David's birth and death on Shavuot.

After Shavuot, the festival cycle takes a break which allowed the first-century populace to tend their crops during the busy growing season. The next round of festivals come in the fall of the year after the harvest. Pilgrimage is then made to Jerusalem for Sukkot, the Feast of Tabernacles.

Part II
The Feasts of The Fall Harvest

The Cycle of Rehearsals Yet To Be fulfilled

The Old Testament is a divinely inspired historical account of man on earth that continually repeats itself. If you want to know what God is doing at any given time, you will find a like scenario in the pages of the First Covenant, and can follow its conclusion to know what will follow. Therefore, it stands to reason that the lives of the Patriarchs mirror our own spiritual journeys.

Let's explore the richness, heritage, and lessons of the Fall Pilgrimage Feasts, and discover what Christians can learn from taking a closer look and finding deeper meaning. Common practices among the modern Jewish community during their holidays hold a hidden richness for us.

The holidays are called *Moedim* in Hebrew, having a connotation of a rehearsal. Each of these holidays are, in fact, just that, a rehearsal for an end time event. Some have already been fulfilled while others portray the wrap-up of the ages and the coming of the Messiah to redeem His own.

It was not until the 3rd century A.D. that the formal church council of Rome passed laws forbidding church members to observe the Levitical festivals. By that time the Church had divorced itself from its Hebraic roots.

Only in recent times are we seeing a desire to fully understand these Feasts of the Lord and participate in the celebrations.

Rosh
Hashana
The
Feast
of Trumpets

The Fall Festivals begin with Rosh Hashana. Because the Jewish festival calendar is based on a lunar cycle, the exact date shifts from year to year on the Roman calendar. Generally the holiday falls in September or October.

Rosh Hashana is the Jewish "New Year" and means literally, the "head of the year." Those well-versed in the Scriptures will realize that this does not follow the scriptural tenet. Rosh Hashana is the beginning of the *civil cycle* as opposed to the *spiritual cycle*. The spiritual cycle falls in the Jewish calendar month of Aviv, in the spring, with Passover.

Among the Jewish people it is thought that Rosh Hashana is a celebration of the creation of the world. Therefore, the spiritual cycle's beginning in the month of Aviv could be viewed as God interfacing with man and the celebration of its beginning.

The Torah Reading Cycle

On Shabbat, (Saturday, the Jewish Sabbath), in every synagogue, several men are called up to participate in a reading from the Torah, one of the first five books of Moses. The five books are broken up into a 52-portion cycle, one for each week of the year and each bearing its own distinctive name.

In every synagogue world-wide, the identical Torah portion is being read and studied. Each of these Torah portions are supplemented with a reading from the prophets. This section is called the *Haf-Torah* portion and in theme, it augments the portion from the Torah reading.

Sacrifice Your Son, Your Only Son

The Akedah

There are two portions read during Rosh Hashana in the synagogue. The first portion details the birth of Isaac. The second portion is called the "*Akedah,*" literally meaning "binding." This Genesis chapter 22 account records for us the long journey of Abraham, his two servants, and his son to a place three days journey from his home, which ended in the binding of Isaac for the required sacrifice.

It was a solemn journey. From the beginning there was no guessing about what they were going to do - wood was taken, fire was carried in the traditional manner in an earthenware vessel. Strangely, no sacrificial animal accompanied them. Isaac's questioning of his father deepens the pathos of the story. Abraham, in obedience to God's request, prepares to sacrifice his only son.

> *Early the next morning Abraham got up and saddled his donkey. He took with him two of his servants and his son Isaac. When he had cut enough wood for the burnt offering, he set out for the place God had directed him to. On the third day, Abraham looked up and saw the place in the distance. He said to his servants, "Stay here with the donkey while I and the boy go over there. We will worship and then we will come back to you."*

> *Abraham took the wood for the burnt offering and placed it on his son Isaac, and he himself carried the fire and the knife. As the two of them went on together, Isaac spoke up and said to his father Abraham,*
>
> *"Father?"*
>
> *"Yes, my son?" Abraham replied.*
>
> *"The fire and the wood are here," Isaac said, "but where is the lamb for the burnt offering?"*
>
> *Abraham answered, "God Himself will provide the lamb for the burnt offering, my son." And the two of them went on together.*

The power of the story is not actually that Abraham was asked by God to sacrifice Isaac, the real power of the story is that God intervened to prevent the sacrifice.

> *Then he reached out his hand and took the knife to slay his son. But the angel of the Lord called out to him from heaven,*
>
> *"Abraham! Abraham!"*
>
> *"Here am I," he replied.*
>
> *"Do not lay a hand on the boy," he said.*
>
> *"Now I know that you fear God, because you have not withheld from me your son, your only son."*
>
> *Abraham looked up and there in a thicket he saw a ram caught by its horns.*

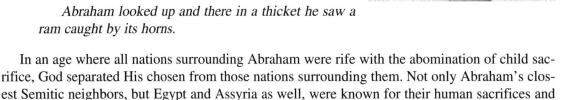

In an age where all nations surrounding Abraham were rife with the abomination of child sacrifice, God separated His chosen from those nations surrounding them. Not only Abraham's closest Semitic neighbors, but Egypt and Assyria as well, were known for their human sacrifices and cruelty to human beings in obedience to their gods.

". . . he saw a ram caught by its horns" - the Hebrew word for *"horns"* is worth investigating. It is the word from which came the erroneous concept that Jewish people have horns. Even Michelangelo in his awe inspiring sculpture of Moses mistakenly placed horns on his head. *Keren*, means "horn" in Hebrew, but it also means "foundation," and "rays of light" among other definitions. Moses came down from the mountain of God radiating light, not with animal-like growths on his head.

The ensuing use of the rams horn, also known as a *shofar*, throughout the ages in Judaism suggests the word "foundation" as well as "glory." The shofar has been used since that time and will be used to culminate the end of the age when we will hear the sounding of the Great Shofar.

The Blowing of The Shofar

An awe-inspiring seasonal practice which is echoed in teachings of the New Testament, is the blowing of a trumpet-like instrument called a *shofar*. The shofar is a ram's horn hollowed out to create a crude musical instrument. Actually, in the Bible, Rosh Hashana is called *Yom Teruah* meaning the "Day of Sounding the Shofar." It is also called *Yom ha Zikkaron* meaning the "Day of Remembering." (Leviticus 23:23-25)

The sounding of the shofar is a kind of spiritual wake-up call. The shofar is rather impressive looking. It serves several purposes. One of those purposes is to remind us of the ram that God provided to be sacrificed in Isaac's stead. The manner in which the shofar is blown is purposeful as well. There are three cycles of sounding of the ram's horn in the Jewish feast, and each has a different meaning. They are listed here:

- The first is called **tekiah**, which means "blast." It is a long, clear note on the shofar that I personally find sends shivers down my spine. The intent is to cause the worshipper to pay attention.

- The second is called **shevarim**, and means "broken." This is three short notes blown together and held to equal the length of the *tekiah* blast above.

- **Teruah** or "alarm," is a rapid series of very short blasts, numbering at least nine, whose duration should also equal one *tekiah*.

- The final sounding of the shofar is called the "**tekiah ha-g'dolah**" and is a long note held out - the duration of which is determined by how much lung power the shofar blower can produce!

In a spiritual sense, the shofar-blowing formula symbolizes the fall of mankind and the world plunged into chaos as a result. It is to remind us of our sinful nature and our need for the provision of our Creator, through the blood of the sacrifice, to make us whole again. The final, symbolic, conclusion of the shofar blowing is encouraging as it announces to us that the broken world is made whole again - and the ram's horn is the instrument by which we are reminded of God's redeeming plan to bring healing to a broken world, through His great mercy.

Redemption echoes from thousands of years back to our father Abraham and his obedience. In an interesting note on the subject - Rabbi Isaiah Horowitz in the 17th century wrote in his book, The Two Tablets of the Covenant, that each series of shofar blasts begins and ends with a *tekiah* (a long continuous note). These are like parentheses to the broken blasts. Therefore, the theme of Rosh Hashana is, "We were whole, we became broken, but we shall be whole again."

As believers in Yeshua the Messiah, we are awaiting the sounding of the last trumpet (shofar) to announce His coming. The Bible is filled with descriptions of this event. The Scriptures liken it to a harvest, in fact, the "final" harvest. When you hear the blowing of a shofar, it is an arresting of one's spirit that creates a sense of alertness. When that "Great Trumpet" sounds, signaling the coming of the Messiah and the end of time as we know it, I'm sure we will recognize it as a heavenly shofar blast that points to God's chosen, eternal sacrifice, the Lamb upon the Throne. All the earth will come up to worship Him.

Adonai Yireh

God's revealed name in the story of Abraham is *Adonai-Yireh*, meaning "God will see to it," (i.e., God will provide). It is humbling to read that Abraham worshiped God even though what was required of him became his greatest trial. Abraham responds to the Lord by saying, "*Hineni*" meaning "Here am I, Lord" (Genesis 23:11). He did not just respond with a nod of the head or a verbal acknowledgement that he had heard, but with this word, "I am at your service." The Hebrew language records that Abraham bowed low before the Lord in submission and adoration. The Hebrew word used there is *"hishtachaveh"* and is described in other places as "an act which bends a man double." We understand this as bowing in a posture of deepest worship in total submission to God.

At this point, Abraham chose to obey the Lord, even though it would mean the greatest loss in his life, his only son. It put in immediate jeopardy God's promise to bless the people of the earth through him and his offspring. Somehow, faith superceded the flood of doubts that surely came to overwhelm him. God revealed Himself, *Adonai Yireh*, "God will provide" (Genesis 23:14). Abraham chose to trust his God and so he remains for us an enduring example of a man of great faith.

The captivating drama given to us in the story of Isaac's binding is filled with lessons: how to hear the voice of God, how to respond to the voice of God, how to worship when all within you wants to turn the other way and not obey. This point of biblical history is pivotal - the turning point for all humanity, for all time. This lesson deserves to be celebrated. One can not learn it by celebrating for only one season. This is undoubtedly why God told the Israelites to celebrate the biblical feasts annually. Each year God's people are in a different place (whether a physical location or just emotionally), and will see these truths of God with fresh eyes as applications to be appropriated in our lives. It will constantly be a new opportunity to trust God no matter how difficult. These lessons just keep being unveiled. Our family has kept the Fall Festivals for almost 20 years and I never tire of it. The Lord continues to reveal Himself to me as *Adonai Yireh*.

The Sacrificial Lamb

It is interesting that the scriptural focus of Rosh Hashana is an animal, biblically prescribed for sacrifice. In contrast we remember the golden calf in the wilderness and the Israelites traveling through a "crucible" (the desert) which in effect, God used to forge them into a nation rather than just a group of people living together in a foreign land.

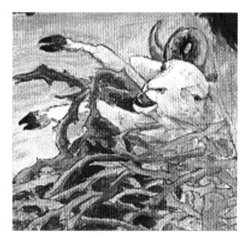

The "golden calf" encounter was almost spiritual death. In fact, it got an immediate response from God. In direct opposition to that, Abraham's encounter was a road-sign to life, a pointer to a future series of events that would mean redemption for the world. Abraham remains God's example of a worshipper with a heart of faith, for the Jewish people to pattern their lives after, each New Year.

God's provision of a ram for sacrifice was "life from the dead," a prophetic example pointing down the ages to the Messiah. I am sure Abraham considered his son as good as dead - but he was willing to offer his "best" to the Lord.

I often wonder about Abraham's thoughts enroute to sacrifice his son. I am sure those thoughts are much like ours - "What did I do that was so bad that my son would need to be sacrificed?" he must have thought. While we focus on one square inch, God sees the entire universe. Abraham could not have known that God was dividing time and space, people from people, the faithful from the faithless, for all of eternity in one heart-rending event.

There were very specific instructions to the Israelites as they brought their sacrifices to be offered before the Lord. Not just any animal would do; it had to be a perfect one, without spot or blemish. Through the sacrifice of this animal, the sins of the worshipper would be transferred and thereby atoned for, satisfying the law of God.

The Book of Life

It is from the Jews that we inherit the knowledge that God keeps a scroll called "The Book of Life." Daniel 12:1 says:

"*. . . but, at that time everyone whose name is found written in the book will be delivered.*" With that in mind, traditional Hebrew greetings during Rosh Hashana are more understandable. "*Shana tovah, tikateivu!*" meaning, "May your name be inscribed for a good year." People also greet each other with, "*Kitevah tovah*" or a "good inscription in the Book of Life."

One of the delicious traditions of the season is the dipping of apple slices in honey to allow the partaker, in some small way, to taste the sweetness of the coming year. When you go to the home of a friend you will often be greeted with sliced apples and a bowl of honey. Together you partake with the blessing on your lips and in your heart that each may know the blessings of God upon their lives in the coming year. The most heartfelt prayer for family and loved ones is that they would be found acceptable in the eyes of God to be inscribed forever in His Book of Life.

Rosh Hashana is unlike any of Israel's other holy days in that it ends in a bittersweet preparation for Yom Kippur. The Day of Atonement is the most solemn day in the Jewish calendar. The ten days between Rosh Hashana and Yom Kippur are called the Days of Awe.

Return O Israel To The Lord Your God

The Days of Awe

During the ten days between Rosh Hashana and Yom Kippur, the Jewish people spend serious time in spiritual introspection, and so it has come to be known as the Days of Awe. Restitution is a part of this preparation. It is the act of making wrong things right, and of going to those you know you have wronged with apologies, even when it seems hard to do. Unfortunately, restitution is a subject not talked about enough in Christian circles, but it is vital during the repentance process.

I have seen marriage partners here that were about to break up, get back together again. During this time, people pay off debts and make apologies to business partners. As Christians, who would fashion their lives after the character of God, we should live our lives in *awe* constantly - on a daily basis - in awe of His power and authority - in awe of His love and mercy. It is living our lives in godly reverence, walking before Him carefully, walking truthfully with each other, and extending mercy at every opportunity.

S'lihot Prayers

During the "Days of Awe" there are special prayers called *S'lihot Prayers* (the meaning in Hebrew is "forgive me.") These are coupled with a ceremony called *Tashlich* (from the Hebrew verb "to throw"), in which bread crumbs or small stones are cast into a body of water to symbolize God casting our sins into the deepest sea. Bread crumbs have leaven which has always symbolized sin in Scripture. Stones might suggest the weight with which sin burdens one down. God has promised that He will cast our sins into the sea to be forever forgotten.

> *You will again have compassion on us; You will tread our sins underfoot and hurl*
> *all our iniquities into the depths of the sea.*   Micah 7:19

Perhaps, similar to what we see here, John the Baptist was encouraging his followers to bring forth fruits worthy for repentance. In other words, acts of love shown by the forgiven sinner, who has decided to return to God's ways, become proof of the repentant heart. It is interesting to note that in the great revivals of the Church, repentance and restitution were always hallmarks of the worshipper, and clearly led the way for a fresh outpouring of the Spirit of God upon His people.

Yom Kippur
A Time of Covering

He will cover you
with His feathers,
and under His wings
you will find refuge;
His faithfulness
will be your
shield and rampart.

Psalm 91:4

Day of Atonement

Yom Kippur is one of the most amazing days of the Hebrew calendar. To experience Yom Kippur in Israel is truly an awe-inspiring time. You really sense the nation of Israel very quiet before God. There is a holy hush that descends over the country. You also sense the Lord Himself hovering over the land.

Living in Israel has made Yom Kippur much more meaningful to my family. Everything stops in Israel on Yom Kippur several hours before sundown. (Remember, that a day in Israel is from sundown to sundown as described in Genesis.) There are no radios, no televisions, no phone calls, and all businesses are closed. It is even true that there are no automobiles running on that day. My children loved Yom Kippur as they grew up here. No cars on the street meant it was the one day out of the year that you could bike or skate or just take a walk right down the *middle* of the street! Thousands of Israelis are out walking in the streets for hours after the synagogue services are over. Then the city becomes very, very quiet for the remainder of this solemn day.

It is truly a day of observance to all of Israel as they contemplate the seriousness of their sinful condition. Many will do an absolute fast for 24 hours - no food and no water. This is very difficult in the hot, arid climate of Israel. Even leather shoes are not worn, as in times past leather was considered to be a luxury. The directive from Leviticus 23 is to "deny yourselves." My family and I spend the day in thanksgiving for what God has done in our lives and how He has provided an atonement for sin, and in intercession for the people of Israel as they direct their hearts toward God on this day.

The sacrifice on the Day of Atonement, in biblical times, required that the sinner join the priest offering the sacrifice by putting his hands on the head of the animal being offered up. We now live in a world hardened to the reality of death by too much violence on television. Then people were tender and the act of placing one's hands on the head of his sacrifice and feeling the life drain out of the animal must have been a trauma, underscoring the price of sin in a way that no other act could. Sin must not have seemed so trivial. Even today, Judaism is convinced of the need for blood sacrifice. The open market in Jerusalem's central section provides stalls for a man called a *"Shochet."* The Orthodox family purchases a chicken and the *shochet* slaughters the chicken in front of the family in a ceremony of repentance. They know there is need for a covering.

Yom Kippur is a day of making reconciliation with God for sins committed during the previous year. The Day of Atonement, or maybe better yet, "At-one-ment" (if looked at analytically), stood out above all the others as a day when one was serious about reflecting on his spiritual life and lifestyle. For believers in Messiah, this Levitical calendar day does not hold dread but an opportunity for thanksgiving that the Most Holy Place is open to us to come into the Shekinah Presence of the Lord God Almighty. (Heb. 10:19-23)

The Covering

Exploring some of the characteristics of Yom Kippur prove to be revealing of the character of God. The word *kippur* means "covering" in Hebrew. Below are some other words that come from this same verb that will enhance our understanding:

- **Kippa** - the small head covering worn by religious Jewish men.
- **Caper** - shelter, as in Capernaum, (i.e. the "shelter of Nahum," the village on the shores of the Galilee).
- **Ha-Kapporet Ha-Zahav** - (In English "Mercy Seat.") The literal Hebrew translation is "the golden covering." This was the lid of solid gold on the Ark of the Covenant over which two golden cherubim spread their wings in covering. When the Ark was finally brought to the Temple, there were two additional cherubim which covered the entire Holy of Holies with their wings.

Throughout the Scriptures we repeatedly see the imagery of covering - i.e. "under the shadow of His wings;" the cherubim who would spread their wings over the "mercy seat" in the Holy of Holies, and the other two cherubim who would overshadow the entire Ark of the Covenant later in the Temple.

As a child I could take just about any piece of cloth or blanket and turn a few chairs over on the dining room floor and make a tent. Crawling into that cozy place was always a special feeling. Hidden away, surrounded by a make-shift security blanket where no one could see me, I felt safe. I loved making a tent. I think most children are the same. There are so many references to being sheltered under the shadow of His wings or being under His covering. Psalm 91 certainly paints that picture for us. I believe as human beings we have a strong emotional desire to return to those tipped-over chairs in the dining room and crawl into the presence of the Lord where we feel sheltered and safe.

> *He who dwells in the shelter of the Most High will rest in the shadow of the Almighty. I will say of the Lord, "He is my refuge and my fortress, my God in whom I trust" . . . He will cover you with His feathers, and under His wings you will find refuge; His faithfulness will be your shield and rampart.*
>
> Psalm 91:1,2,4

"Tryst" is a wonderful literary word. It means a prearranged meeting place and is used most often describing *lovers*. The Lord continually beckons us to come enjoy the "tryst" of prayer, praise and communion with Him. From cover to cover the Bible reveals that God desires intimate fellowship with us. Enfolded in His presence, alone with Him, in devout worship we can please the Lord beyond anything else we can offer. A yielded heart is our daily offering. He desires to make us the recipient of His lavish mercy.

The Priestly Blessing

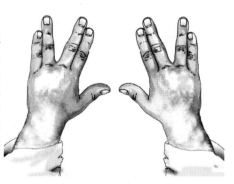

Only on the "Day of Atonement" did the High Priest pronounce the usually unutterable name of God. This was the day when all the people heard the name of God and cried out to Him. On this day when all was forgiven and atoned for, God's name was invoked over His people with great ceremony. The High Priest would form the Hebrew letter *Shin*, the first letter of the Hebrew word "*Shaddai*" meaning Almighty, with his hands. Then lifting his hands, he would pronounce the Aaronic benediction, also known as the Priestly Blessing, over the people.

> *The LORD said to Moses, "Tell Aaron and his sons, 'This is how you are to bless the Israelites. Say to them:*
> *"The LORD bless you and keep you;*
> *The LORD make His face to shine upon you, and be gracious to you;*
> *The LORD lift up His face upon you, and give you peace."'*
> *"So, they will put My name upon the Israelites, and I will bless them."*
>
> Numbers 6:22-27

יברכך יי וישמרך
יאר יי פניו אליך ויחנך
ישא יי פניו אליך וישם לך שלום

69

I believe that this benediction has been adopted by the Church because there is an inherent underlying power in it. That power lies in the fact that God said, *"So, they will put My name upon the Israelites."* The Church recognized that benefit and uses the benediction regularly. Even though this benediction is used in the synagogue more often than once a year now, it echoes back to being "inscribed for a good year" as in ancient times when the Day of Atonement was the once yearly occasion that the Priestly Blessing was formally made over the people. In reality, it was a covering of blessing for the people of the Most High God.

Another noteworthy phrase is: *"...and the LORD lift up His face upon you and give you peace."* This has to be understood from the imagery of a king's court. Never does a king have to have his face "lifted up" upon his subjects, therefore it must mean something else. From other biblical references we find the phrase is understood to mean, *"...and the LORD lift His face upon you* [in a smile] *and give you peace."* (Encyc. Judaica - Priestly blessing.)

It is also interesting to note that just before Jesus ascended into heaven after His resurrection, He *"lifted His hands"* and blessed His disciples.

> When He had led them out to the vicinity of Bethany, He **lifted up His hands** and blessed them. While He was blessing them, He left them and was taken up into heaven. Then they worshiped Him and returned to Jerusalem with great joy.
>
> Luke 24:50

Many Jewish people would automatically know that when a priest or spiritual leader lifts his hands for a blessing, he is pronouncing the Aaronic benediction and thereby invoking the name of God with all the fullness of His blessings upon the people. Could that be why the disciples returned to Jerusalem filled with "great joy" even though they had just bid farewell to their Master?

The Book of Jonah - Gentile Nations

The Synagogue reading for Yom Kippur is the entire book of Jonah. This reading is pointed at Gentiles. God so cared for the Assyrians that He sent one of His chosen prophets to them to tell them to repent. Two hundred years of peace and prosperity followed for the Assyrians due to their willingness to heed God's message. This reading dispels despair when we realize that, like Jonah, our own failure to carry out God's will is not uncommon. The bottom line of the message is not to lose hope.

We can understand Jonah's terror better by comparing today's Baghdad in Iraq with the Assyrian capital city of Nineveh. Nineveh was renowned for its cruelty to its enemies and prisoners of war. Large rings were hooked in the lips or jaws of their captives and they were marched behind horses back to Nineveh where they would possibly be blinded, have their thumbs and large toes cut off, tongues cut out, and be sold into slavery. We can identify with Jonah's fears in light of Nineveh's reputation, but we must also make note of God's mercy, as Nineveh's stay-of-execution shows us.

Just as the story of Abraham is read on Rosh Hashana, and serves as an example of faith, so the book of Jonah is the model of repentance and mercy. This book has great significance on Yom Kippur. God is faithful to Gentile nations when they turn their hearts in true repentance toward Him. He remains forever merciful to all nations.

Nineveh was a great threat to Israel's security. God was protecting His chosen people by commissioning Jonah to deliver His message of repentance. A repentant nation on Israel's northern border was a blessing from God.

But with some nations things may never change. It is interesting that Israel's modern neighbors understood Yom Kippur and took advantage of it. In 1973, Israel's enemies chose to attack Israel at a time when communication was at its lowest. The news of the Yom Kippur War, as it was called, passed by word of mouth from synagogue to synagogue and in the street from person to person as Israel rallied for war to defend herself. A public call to arms was impossible since radio and television stations do not operate on Yom Kippur. As mentioned previously, automobiles are prohibited from driving on Yom Kippur in the Jewish State of Israel.

It seems that God always rallies with Israel when she is attacked - Israel won the war and took possession of the entire Sinai from Egypt, and the Golan Heights from Syria, very similar to when Israel was spared from those who would have attacked her in centuries past.

In a similar unprovoked attack six years earlier called "The Six Day War," Jordan lost the West Bank and the city of Jerusalem. Jordan viewed Jerusalem and Israel as "greater Jordan" between the years of 1948 and 1967. It is interesting that until the signing of the Peace agreement between Israel and Jordan that Jordan's TV weather map did not even acknowledge that Israel existed. The nation of Jordan extended all the way to the Mediterranean. When temperatures were given, a beautiful picture of the Dome of the Rock was shown and the title was "The Western Heights." The late King Hussein of Jordan had been building a second palace on the hills about three miles north of Jerusalem prior to the "Six Day War." It still sits there where its construction was arrested by his unexpected loss of portions of Israel.

One will find people staring into the sky after sundown on Shabbat or any Jewish holiday. They are looking for three stars in one glance - the same is true on Yom Kippur. The sighting of three visible stars in one glance in the evening sky means that the holy day has come to an end. With the sighting, Yom Kippur is officially over.

71

Families gather after the synagogue service to partake of a meal to break the fast, but within a few hours hammering will begin. Almost in a rush to begin "rejoicing" many begin to build their tabernacles in which to celebrate Sukkot. That evening, fathers and sons join together industriously and work far into the night in preparation for the next eight days of celebration, while mothers and daughters are busy preparing decorations and planning meals.

Sukkot

The Feast of
Tabernacles

The Season of Our Rejoicing

Sukkot (the Feast of Tabernacles) is probably the most important of the Pilgrimage Festivals. The Hebrew term "*He Hag*" (meaning "The Feast") is so well understood that all Jewish people know that you are referring to Sukkot when you say it. In Jewish tradition this holiday is also called, "the season of our rejoicing."

The cycle of fall feast days describes a progressive process whose intent is to illustrate how God covers us spiritually at Yom Kippur, and physically during the Feast of Tabernacles. There is a marked contrast now, moving away from the solemnity of Yom Kippur to Sukkot's rejoicing attitude. Actually, this is the only feast at which the Israelites are commanded to be filled with joy. Deuteronomy 16:14 says, "*. . . Be joyful at your feast - you, your sons and daughters, your menservants and maidservants, and the Levites, the aliens, the fatherless and the widows who live in your towns.*" They understand the directive to set aside all sorrow and take joy in the Lord.

The Israelites were directed to build a tabernacle (sukka) in which to dwell for seven days. The week was to be a memorial of times past in which God led His children through the wilderness from Egypt to the promised land. According to Zech. 14:16, all nations of the world will one day come up to Jerusalem to keep the Feast of Tabernacles.

The Levitical Feasts revolve around an agricultural motif, as communities thousands of years ago were able to identify with these mental images readily. Even if a man was not a farmer, he could easily understand agricultural terminology.

Since the feasts of the book of Leviticus are calculated by a lunar calendar, according to the book of Genesis, the moon functions as the time clock dictating festival times. Sukkot is an attempt to relive the journey through the wilderness with the children of Israel. The hope is that we will be able to apply these biblical lessons to our lives.

A sukka (tabernacle or booth), is the structure in which the Jewish people celebrate the holiday. It consists of three walls, usually covered on the sides with cloth. The inside is decorated with fruits of the harvest and colorful hand-made items usually crafted by the children of the household. In Orthodox families, all meals are eaten in the sukka for the seven-day period. In Conservative homes, some meals are taken in the sukka.

The most interesting part of the sukka is the roof. People scour the city for tree branches. In fact, the date farmers take this holiday as an opportunity to trim their date-palms and provide the palm branches for roofing material. The rule is, that you must be able to see the stars through the branches of the roof.

Qumran and the Sukka

One of our family Sukkot celebrations may illustrate the picture better for you. Some of us who live in Israel try to go to the desert by the shores of the Dead Sea on the eve of Sukkot.

It is generally very hot in Israel for the first few days of Sukkot. For the harvest festivals, the moon always rises over the Jordan Valley and Dead Sea majestically. For those bold enough to actually go down to the desert and brave the intense heat for the first night of Sukkot, the shimmering, orange harvest moon puts on an incredible show. On this occasion it was full and glorious. It just seems to take its time on the eve of Sukkot illuminating both the night sky and the absolutely glass-smooth surface of the Dead Sea in dark gold. It doesn't seem real - a panorama of biblical proportions. It seems not to want to hurry the once-a-year event, but rather to savor it and give as much of itself as possible to the celebrants. Amazingly, it seems to know how special the event is as it slowly rides the atmosphere up the heavens.

We spend hours there, singing and celebrating, along with thousands of other celebrants who come up yearly to worship the Lord during the Feast of Tabernacles. This Dead Sea event is the opening night of the International Christian Embassy's Sukkot annual celebration.

Later, back at home, the warm weather beckoned me to sleep outside in our sukka that we build every year on our front balcony. The moon wasn't finished with its production. Now, high enough in the sky to be a brilliant silver orb washing the color from everything, it did a dance across the lacy top of our sukka, ducking in and out between the slats and branches. The moon was so bright that it hid most of the stars. It seemed to demand the respect of all around it. It was hard to get to sleep. Carol, my wife, and I just lay there taking in the wonder and reminiscing about past years in our family sukka. There are few times in life when one is given the opportunity to relive childhood and build a ramshackle structure that threatens to fall down if a serious wind came along.

I recall a newspaper article several years ago about some Jewish students at an American university asking permission to build a "sukka" on campus. The administration finally agreed since it was a religious observance, but then overturned their consent a few days later when they viewed the instability of the structure and deemed it "unsafe." I wonder what they would have "deemed" safe had they been crossing the Sinai with Moses and the children of Israel? Remember, the sukka is supposed to be a simple structure and covered with just enough branches to allow you to see the sky and the spectacle that it presents during this month of the year. It is to be a visible reminder of the temporary dwellings of the Israelites in the desert enroute to a permanent dwelling place.

The Festival of Sukkot is designed to give us a platform in which to give thanks to God for the last harvest of the year, similar to the *Thanksgiving* holiday in America. It is also meant to be a reminder of our frailty living here on planet earth. It is a replay, if you will, of the time in the desert when the construction of a booth for shelter from the hot sun was all one had. Remember, even though the final lap in the wilderness was in tents, the Israelites did not leave Egypt equipped with tents. They began that time in booths with branches probably gathered from the rivers closer to Egypt where there was an abundance of reeds. Tent making obviously matured while in the wilderness.

The Wilderness

A visiting pastor here spoke about Egypt and the "wilderness experience." We sometimes refer to being in the "wilderness" when we feel we are not experiencing the presence of the Lord as we think we should, or wish we could. But remember, it was in the wilderness that God could be "seen" most clearly - in His provision of manna, in the cloud by day and the pillar of fire by night, in the mountain that thundered and the ring of clouds covering the summit. Also, in the clothes and shoes that never wore out, even after 40 years. Rough and rudimentary conditions in that wilderness mean that we are totally dependent on His provision for our every need. We experience His Presence without distraction.

It would probably be more appropriate, when faced with a time that you don't sense the presence of the Lord, to say that you have been "left back in Egypt," where the beggarly grave clothes of slavery and a life filled with distractions get in the way of experiencing His presence. At times, abundance is not a good thing. Remember, the children of Israel were tempted to return to the leeks and garlic of the "good life" in Egypt. They literally craved them. How quickly they forgot the reality of Egyptian life.

As we touched on before, the life of the Hebrews in Egypt was likely not slavery as we think of slavery. They were certainly a servant-class, but many indications are available to estimate that it was a fairly exalted class distinction, at least up to the last years of their existence there.

So, the slaves of Egypt were not necessarily poor - they came out of Egypt with vast wealth, enough to build the tabernacle. The Egyptians also contributed to the Israelites with a "going away gift" as they pleaded with them to leave Egypt.

There are two books dealing with the wilderness experience that I highly suggest. They have brought the wilderness to life for me. Jamie Buckingham's books, <u>A Way Through The Wilderness</u>, and <u>Where Eagles Soar</u> portray the Sinai Desert as being the place of God's discipline in order to prepare His people, as well as the place of His presence and provision. The desert provides a hearty learning experience.

The Festive Feast

We are commanded several things about the Festival of Tabernacles - but the most important thing is to be joyful. Amazing, is it not? No other festival has such a directive. BE JOYFUL! No mourning allowed. This feast stands as a rehearsal for the final harvest when all things will be finished and we will behold the face of the "Desire of the Ages," our Messiah, and will sit down with Him at the Wedding Supper of the Lamb. The picture of being under the "covering" for seven days in joyful celebration is very descriptive of a biblical wedding feast.

It is also incumbent upon those celebrating the feast to "dwell" in the booth for seven days. That has come to mean at least partaking of some meals in the booth. Sitting down to a meal in biblical times meant so much more than just sitting down to eat with your family. It was precursor to a covenant - sometimes between men and sometimes with God, but always with the intent of reconciliation between both parties. What a picture. Under the "covering" of the sukka, we "partake" of a covenant meal, festively, for seven days with the command of our God to "Be joyful!"

Back to our family Sukkot story - inside the sukka on our balcony, Carol and I finally drifted off to sleep. She told me when I awoke the next morning that she had been awakened at 5:00 am for a further spectacle. The moon was finally finishing its "feast dance" and sinking in the west in another blaze of golden glory. Our apartment, high on a hill in south Jerusalem, faces southeast toward the desert. On the eastern horizon, from somewhere out in the desert, a plume of smoke was rising. The air was so absolutely still that the plume was as straight as if it had been drawn with a ruler, rising over the desert floor like the "cloud by day" must have appeared. It seemed a gentle reminder of a long ago wilderness trek where you could "see" God's greatness with your own eyes.

Build Your Own Sukka

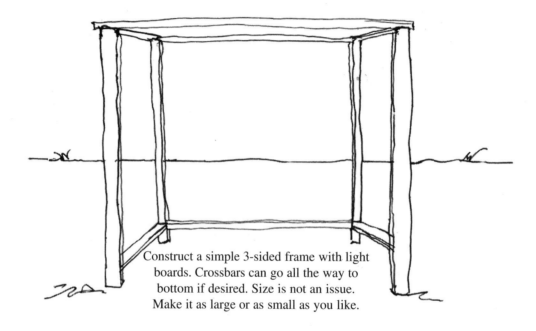

Construct a simple 3-sided frame with light
boards. Crossbars can go all the way to
bottom if desired. Size is not an issue.
Make it as large or as small as you like.

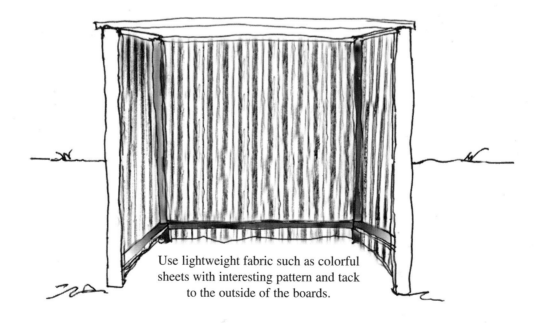

Use lightweight fabric such as colorful
sheets with interesting pattern and tack
to the outside of the boards.

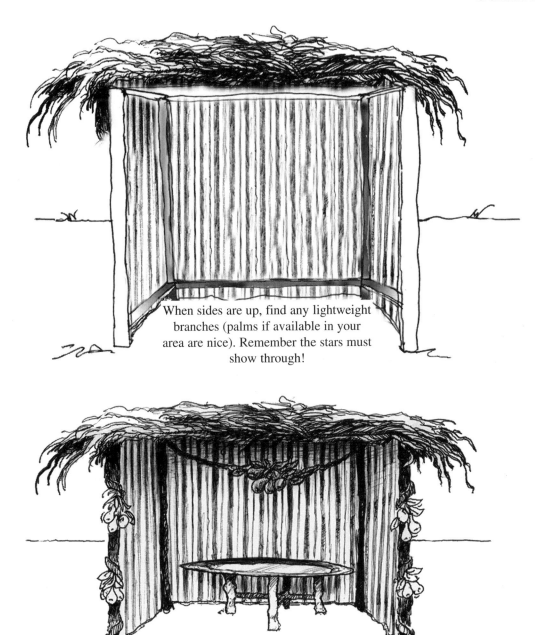

When sides are up, find any lightweight
branches (palms if available in your
area are nice). Remember the stars must
show through!

Decorate with colorful fruit of the season;
even plastic shiny decorations help make it
festive looking. Place table, chairs, and
pillows inside to make it comfortable.

79

The Four Species

Leviticus 23:40 also describes another exercise of applied thankfulness during Sukkot - the Israelites were to take the branches of three types of trees and the produce of "goodly trees" and wave them before the Lord as a thank offering. These are commonly known as the "Four Species."

On the first day you shall take the product of goodly trees, branches of palm trees, boughs of leafy trees, and willows of the brook, and you shall rejoice before the Lord your God seven days.

The product of goodly trees is symbolized by a lemon-like fruit called the *etrog*. In some places it is called a citron. The boughs of trees are respectively - palm branch (called a *lulav*), Myrtle (called *hadasim*), and willows (called *aravot*). These items were to be held aloft and waved in the four directions of the compass: north, south, east, and west.

The strange looking fruit is known as the **etrog**

Some commentaries see these "Four Species," as being like four types of people. The **etrog** has a lemon fragrance and taste. This is like the man who possesses spiritual understanding and follows it up with actions that display his spiritual life. The **palm tree** has taste but no fragrance. This is like the man who possesses spiritual understanding but his life does not exhibit it. The **myrtle** has fragrance, but no taste. This is like the man who does good things but has no knowledge of God in his life. Finally, the **willow** has neither. It represents the man who has no knowledge of God, and displays no acts of kindness or godliness in his life.

It is interesting to note that *Hoshanot* are recited in the synagogue during the seven days of Sukkot. These are Psalms that begin with the word *hoshana* (from which we get our praise word

"*Hosanna*," meaning, "save us"). These elements were common in Israeli worship in Yeshua's day. Palm branches together with "hoshana" psalms echo another special day in the calendar of the life of the Messiah, His triumphal entry into the city of Jerusalem on Palm Sunday.

The Water Libation

These audio-visual aids to our faith don't stop here. During Temple times there was a custom of drawing water from the Gihon spring, near the Temple Mount where the water exits Hezekiah's tunnel, as a "libation" to accompany the offerings. This meant pouring out water before the Lord in joyful expressions of thanksgiving. It was done with great rejoicing and much ceremony. Some resources have detailed a few of the customs during this water ceremony and they say that they even border on riotous. The joy was almost uncontainable. Yeshua's references to "living water flowing out of your innermost being" in John 7:37, would have struck a chord in the hearts of His hearers, bringing back to their minds the joy during the water libation.

Shemini Atzeret, the eighth day of Sukkot, is the great assembly day added on to the feast. It became known as the "Great Day of the Feast." It was on this day that Yeshua declared Himself to be the source of the spring by calling all those who were thirsty to come drink of Him, and announcing that streams of living water would flow from believers. What a statement! This declaration caused those who heard it to proclaim, *"surely this man is the Prophet."* Others declared him the Messiah. (John 7:37-41)

The Jewish people also pray for rain on *Shemini Atzeret*. There are several different descriptions for rain in the Bible including dew, sprinkles, light showers, rain, and heavy rain. One of those, *Geshemi Bracha*, meant "rains of blessing which are plentiful." These prayers are for heavy rain to bring the spring harvest. It is amazing - I have never seen a year where God did not send at least one rain during Sukkot. Please note, it is not necessary to stay in your sukka in the rain. It's hard to "be joyful" while wet and cold!

Festival e-mail?

Different time periods in the history of the Jewish people have added interesting elements to the feast days. During the Babylonian captivity a problem of accurate timing for the celebrations created a unique communication method.

Communication from Jerusalem to Babylon in order to inform the captives in Daniel's time was via mountaintop bonfires. The first bonfire was set on the top of the Mount of Olives. Succeeding bonfires stretched in a chain across the desert to the city of Babylon. The purpose was to let the captives know the exact beginning of the holidays from Jerusalem's remnant. Perhaps we could call it, the first e-mail?

The Feast of Tabernacles awaits its final fulfillment. Sukkot will find its fulfillment in the final trumpet in which all the dead will arise and the final harvest will be gathered in for threshing and separation - the good from the bad.

We will see with our own eyes the coming of the Messiah to redeem the earth's inhabitants who have patiently awaited Him. A cry, long held inside will find release -

" Messiah, Son of David - Hosanna!"

Messiah

We
Await
Your
Return

Simchat Torah

Torah Scrolls are inscribed on animal skins sewn together .

The Value of God's Word

Simchat Torah means "rejoicing in the Torah" or 'rejoicing in the Word of God." On this day, the Scripture reading cycle that we have already discussed in the section on Rosh Hashana is now complete. The last chapter of Deuteronomy is read, but in the same reading the scroll is rerolled and the first portion of Genesis is read. Tradition answers the obvious question as to why this happens. The Jewish people do not want Satan to think that they are joyful that they have completed the reading of the Torah, but just that they are joyful in the fact that they have the Holy Scriptures.

Simchat Torah falls on a different day in Jerusalem than the rest of the world. There were rules about holidays in walled cities. Jerusalem, in antiquity, was a walled city and continues to fall under those customs. Therefore, in Jerusalem, only one day has been added to the end of Sukkot. Shemeni Atzeret and the Simchat Torah celebration fall on the same day. Outside of Jerusalem, Simchat Torah falls on the ninth day.

God's Word Preserved

The holiday pivots around the Word of God. The Scriptures have not always existed in glossy leather bindings. In biblical times, ancient scrolls were made of animal hide and carefully inscribed by learned men called scribes. A scribe's life was dedicated to the accurate recopying of the Word of God. The care and precision of the scribal arts is inspiring. Rules and regulations guided, protected, and guaranteed us a text, intact and anointed by the Spirit of God.

A scribe would pause before penning יהוה - the name of God. He would prepare himself mentally in order that there be no mistakes during the penning of the Holy Name and pause again after the name was completed. Some stories say that the pen nib used to write the name of God was different and kept separate from other pen nibs.

Torah scrolls were not treated as we treat books today. When a book reaches the end of its usefulness today, we may throw it away, or send it to a used bookstore. Torah scrolls were considered to be the living Word of God. Sacred books and scrolls were not allowed to touch the floor and were never discarded. Yeshua said, *"The words that I speak to you, they are spirit and they are life"* (John 6:63). That statement underscores Jewish concern for the Scriptures. When a Torah scroll has reached the end of its usefulness, it is actually entombed in a special room in the synagogue called the *"geniza."* Usually many scrolls can be found in a synagogue *geniza.* One of the largest repositories of these scrolls was found in Alexandria, Egypt.

The Wedding

Ceremony surrounds the life of a Torah scroll like parentheses. One at the beginning with a distinctive wedding flavor, the other at the end of its life like a burial ceremony. The reception ceremony for a new Torah scroll (the wedding) is called *Hachnasat Sefer Torah.* Our own neighborhood has just had ceremonies for the welcoming of two new Torah scrolls to synagogues close to us. Both of these events captured the attention of the entire neighborhood. First, a Sephardic synagogue of French-speaking immigrants received a new scroll. The congregation sent out invitations for the neighborhood to come and celebrate. There was wonderful music. Tables were set out laden with refreshments. Hundreds of people attended. The male members surrounded their new scroll and danced for hours while the women encouragingly supported from the side. The Torah Scroll is always referred to in the feminine gender. It then begins to be understandable why the celebration is more like a wedding ceremony and reception.

The second Torah scroll received a much more grandiose reception. Police began to gather hours before a carefully planned parade through our neighborhood. They would accompany the parade, assuring the safety of all the celebrants. A great number of men from this Ashkenazi synagogue gathered around an automobile which had been equipped with a large similitude of a king's crown bolted to the roof. Hassidic music played from loud speakers, and probably 100 or more men and boys, some with large blazing torches headed up a long parade route following a *chuppa* (a prayer shawl tacked to four tall poles to create a wedding canopy), with the new scroll under it. Just as in a wedding, the chuppa sheltered the new Torah scroll.

It is such a wondrous thing to see how Israelis' hearts are moved by the Word of God. It is humbling to me to think that entire Jewish communities have sheltered these scrolls, many times in periods of trouble or war. At times, communities have lost lives to preserve these scrolls. I acutely recognize a verse in Romans as applying to me.

For if the Gentiles have shared in the Jews' spiritual blessings, they owe it to the Jews to share with them their material blessings.   Romans 15:27

We as believers have certainly benefited - I speak as a Gentile - and do indeed owe a debt to the Jewish people for their tenacious preservation of God's word and delivering it safely to us. The discovery of the Dead Sea Scrolls underscores this point. Two incidents illustrate the preciousness of these ancient texts.

The Baghdad Mezuzah

I was shopping for a few last-minute gifts to bring to the U.S. with me as I was preparing to go on a speaking tour. Joseph and Jackie, two Armenian Christian brothers that have an antiquities shop in the Old City of Jerusalem, are close friends and very special to us.

I frequent their shop, when I can, just to have coffee and discuss world situations. Their father died a year and a half ago, and their brother Jimmie recently died also. They have adopted me as their *Abba* (meaning Dad). They call me *Abu-George.* The father in a Middle Eastern family takes on the name of the oldest son with the prefix, *Abu* (Arabic form of father). George is their oldest brother, who is now living in the United States.

Sitting with them, we were interrupted by an Arab man peddling antiquities. Joseph stepped aside to talk with him and they began pulling things out of bags and inspecting them carefully. Joseph picked up a strange object that looked like a very old, hand-rolled cigar. Out of a small opening in the back of the cigar-like object, he pulled another piece of material and unrolled it. They discussed it in Arabic and then Joseph handed it to me and asked if I knew what it was.

87

On the small piece of material was written in Hebrew, *"Sh'ma Israel, Adonai Elohenu, Adonai Echad,"* which says, "Hear O Israel, the LORD our God, the LORD is One." It was the small scroll carefully written by a Hebrew scribe and rolled tightly to place inside the Jewish door post adornment called a *mezuzah*. The Jewish people take the directive to place the mezuzah on their doorposts from the Scripture in Deuteronomy 6:4, which says, *"write them on the doorframes of your houses and on your gates"* (meaning, "gates of your city").

The small scroll's scriptural content goes on to direct us to *". . . love the Lord your God with all your heart, with all your soul, with all your strength. . . . write them upon the doorframes of your houses and your gates."* (Deut. 6:4-8)

I have seen plenty of mezuzah scrolls - this one was different. I could tell that this one was by the hand of a scribe, written on animal skin, and also very old. The calligraphy was distinctively from the east and not typically European. The top of the scroll was burned and ragged. The holder itself, to which the scroll is fastened to the doorpost, was made of crude, aged leather. Beautifully rendered calligraphy on the back of the scroll delineated, exactly according to *halacha* (Jewish codes of conduct), the name of God - *Shaddai* - which is the shortened form of *El Shaddai*, God Almighty.

"How much does he want for the scroll?" I asked Joseph.

"$100," he translated for me.

My heart sank. I wanted that scroll. I felt like I was rescuing a treasure from the hands of someone who really could not appreciate it. Joseph turned and said something to the man in Arabic to which he responded with a scowl and a scornful laugh.
"What did you say to him?" I asked Joseph.

"I told him you would give him $5!" he said.

I desperately threw caution to the wind. "Tell him I'll give him $10 for the scroll," I said. I wanted the scroll badly enough to pay the $100 if I had had it. $10 was the most I could come up with right there.

"$70, the man said."

Sadly, I just had to wave him off and went back to packing up the gifts I had purchased to take to loved ones on my trip to America. The man moved toward the door and said something more to Joseph. Joseph took something from him and turned to me and said, "OK, he says he'll take $10."

I took out $10 and handed it to him - my heart was beating so loudly I was sure he could hear it. He took the $10 and disappeared into the corridors of the Old City.

Joseph told me that the man was from Jordan but regularly goes to Iraq and digs around in obscure villages for antiquities. He had found today's treasure in a small village outside Baghdad, Iraq, in the remains of a destroyed Jewish home with this mezuzah still affixed to the doorpost. He took it off the door to find a buyer in Jordan. No one wanted anything with Hebrew writing on it in Jordan, therefore, he had saved it until he could get to Jerusalem where he knew he would find a buyer.

The real clincher, Joseph told me after the man had left, is that he thought the writing on the scroll was a note telling where the Jewish family had hidden their riches. I laughed at such an absurd idea, until I took the scroll to another antiquities dealer to authenticate its age and price. He told me that Iraqi Jewish families had to leave Iraq many times with just the clothing on their backs and did indeed hide family riches thinking they would probably return in a few months. Most of those families who fled never returned. I learned that many of the Iraqi Jewish communities were not poor, though. For instance, a recognizable name - the Sassons were quite wealthy and influential in Iraq.

If the Arab peddler only knew the riches of that little scroll. A tradition of love nailed to the doorposts of Jewish homes world-wide.

I now hold in my hand an antique treasure - a small vignette from one of the communities of Jewish people who paid a price to safeguard the Scriptures for the world.

I wondered how it got burned.

High-Tech Security

It brings to mind a humorous incident when an American company was recording a video and music project here.

The sound engineers were using *Jerusalem Studios* (Israel's television and radio studios) to view and edit tape for the video. Several of them were having a short early morning standup meeting in front of the lobby elevators before they scattered to their respective jobs.

In Israel, nearly every doorpost, both inside and outside, has a mezuzah attached to it. It is Jewish custom to lightly touch the mezuzah with your fingertips as you enter a door and then kiss your finger tips in reverence to the name of God inscribed on the small scroll inside. You will even find a mezuzah on each elevator door. Many people, coming to work that morning, were pausing at the elevator and touching the doorpost then lightly kissing their fingertips before entering the elevator.

One of the group watched out of the corner of his eye for a long time, then could not go any longer without commenting. "You know," he said, "I think that this thing (pointing to the mezuzah) is a very high-tech security device!"

If he only knew the high-tech quality of that "device." God's Word, the treasure beyond all earthly treasures. We are rich beyond all comprehension if we take time to correctly analyze our heritage.

500 year old Iraqi scroll of the book of Esther.

My Iraqi antiquities source has not dried up yet. Several months later I was able to purchase another wonderful piece of history. This one is a 500 year old Iraqi scroll of the entire book of Esther. These scrolls are called "*Megillat Esther*" simply meaning, the "scroll of Esther." It stops me in my tracks to think that as antiquities go, 500 years is rather young and yet America was some 250 years from being founded.

There is just such richness surrounding the history of our Bible. These are lessons that have helped me carry my Bible in a new way. These lessons have helped me not take for granted the leather bound book I have a right to carry so proudly.

Zechariah and King Solomon Saw You

One day, according to Zechariah, all the earth will come up to Jerusalem to keep the Feast of Tabernacles. Rabbis here in Jerusalem have commented on the fact that as thousands of Christians, from around the world, come yearly to celebrate the Feast of Tabernacles, this marks the beginning of Zechariah's prophecy.

> *Then the survivors from all the nations that have attacked Jerusalem will go up year after year to worship the King, the LORD Almighty, and to celebrate the Feast of Tabernacles. If any of the people of the earth do not go up to Jerusalem to worship the King, the LORD God Almighty, they will have no rain.*   Zech. 14:16-17

I always love to share II Chronicles 6 with visitors to Jerusalem. It records King Solomon's dedication of the newly built Temple. Thousands of years ago he looked down the ages and saw us Gentiles, who are not of the commonwealth of Israel; he saw us coming to the Land to worship the God of Israel, because of God's great Name.

> *As for the **foreigner** who does not belong to Your people Israel but has come from a distant land because of Your great name and Your mighty hand and Your outstretched arm - when he comes and prays toward this temple, then hear from heaven, Your dwelling place, and do whatever the foreigner asks of You, so that all the peoples of the earth may know Your name and fear You, as do Your own people Israel, and may know that this house that I have built bears Your Name.*   II Chron. 6:32,33

The entire chapter is a glorious prayer of power and anointing. Then, there is recorded the wonderful request of God to answer, *"whatever the foreigner asks of you . . ."* a testimony for all time.

Two things happen when a believer comes to Israel to "see where it all happened." We are all part of the "bride of Christ." It only makes sense that the fiancé of the bride-to-be would want to show his espoused where he grew up, and introduce her to his family members - like any man in love. Therefore, a wonderful umbrella covers a pilgrim here. I personally love to be with first timers just to see what special thing God is going to do for them while they visit the land.

The second thing is King Solomon's request that God answer the prayer of the foreigner. It is like a blank check. I love to take the Bible and open it to that chapter while showing people around at the Western Wall. I read it and I see the illumination light up their faces. It is then with real power and authority that they approach the Wall where prayer is offered, knowing that God knew they were coming and wanted to meet them there.

Feasts of the LORD

A fringe benefit of these festivals today is that representatives of all nations come here to Israel. God reveals Himself to them, allows them to see the great things He has done for His people, and then they return home to their own country where they cannot help but share their experiences with just about everybody - with their family, at work, on the street, and so many other places. Therefore, the second part of that prayer of King Solomon comes into being. *". . . so that all the peoples of the earth may know Your name and fear You, as do Your own people Israel . . ."* A glorious symbiosis, God and us in partnership, to show the world that He alone is sovereign.

One of those representatives just made a statement that found its way to the Jerusalem Post, our English language newspaper here in Israel. It is well worth quoting. Argentinean football star, Maradona was interviewed and talked about how, before four separate World Cup Tournaments, he flew to Israel to pray at the Western Wall. He said, "I am Catholic, I love Mary and Jesus, but I know that God listens to the Jews. So, I went to Israel to pray because I knew God would listen to me among the Jews, at His holy wall."

Do you know what it is for a Jewish person to hear that, the sense of pride it gives them? They think, "If this guy can find something redemptive in my tradition, then why can't I?"

I hope you too will celebrate the Feast of Tabernacles by building a sukka of your own, eating meals with your family inside, and enjoying the "spectacle" in the sky through the branches of the roof.

It will be a time of "rejoicing" in your God during these festive eight days, with great thanksgiving for all He has done. This holiday is especially made for the "child at heart." Be joyful!!

Part III
Hanukkah and Purim

For with You is the fountain of life; in Your Light, we see Light.

Psalm 36:9

The time between the Old and the New Testament have erroneously been labeled the silent years. A fictional novel could not hold more intrigue or imaginative narrative than this period. Historians who have not fallen under the "spell of silence" have left us enough information to glean valuable lessons from Hanukkah.

Hanukkah is a story of survival, bravery, overcoming faith, and a sovereign God. These lessons are too rich to ascribe to a silent past. They cry out, of themselves, to be paid attention to. If they had been heeded by the church - needless deaths might have been spared during the Holocaust.

Purim follows in the Spring on the heels of Hanukkah. Purim as well is a story about survival. The thread that binds both stories is God's protection over the Jewish nation, His chosen people. One story takes place in the Diaspora (lands of the Jewish people's dispersal from Israel) and the other takes place in "Greek occupied" Israel. The stories take place hundreds of years apart. Esther is dated approximately 460 B.C. and the saga of the Maccabees - Hanukkah - takes place about 160 B.C.

Both of these stories were dictated to the mind of scribes by God's Holy Spirit, I am sure, to leave us an indelible message. The message is that in the face of enormous odds, with God, we are victorious.

Hanukkah

The Festival of Lights

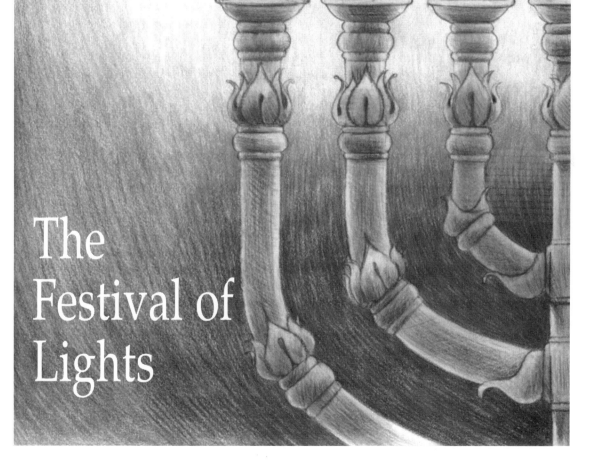

O LORD,
You keep my lamp burning,

You, O my God, turn my
darkness into light.

Psalm 18:28 (Paraphrase)

The Menorah

David Ben Gurion, upon being asked to create a seal for the new State of Israel chose two olive branches surrounding a *menorah*. It stands as the Israeli State Seal to this day. On each of the seven cups of the *menorah* (seven-branched candlestick), is one word. *"Lo b'chil, u'lo b'koach, ki im b'ruachi"* (*"Not by might, nor by power, but by My Spirit says the Lord of hosts"*). This is from Zechariah 4:6 during the time they were rebuilding the Temple after the Babylonian captivity. Remember the word *Hanukkah* in Hebrew simply means "dedication" and specifically refers to the dedication of the Temple of God.

The menorah, stands as a symbol in so many passages of Scripture. Revelation tells us that the seven churches of Asia were represented in the heavenlies by candlesticks. Israel is also represented by the menorah in Zechariah. John, in chapter 9 of his Gospel, records that Jesus is "the light of the world and lights every man." The menorah was meant to bring us light as Israel was meant to be a light to the nations and indeed, did bring forth the Messiah.

Zechariah provides us another interesting tidbit in relation to this as we read further in chapter 4. Zechariah asks about the meaning of the vision of the two olive trees who are pouring oil from themselves. Of course the oil is symbolic of the Holy Spirit of God, but it is interesting to note that in Hebrew it does not say that they were pouring just any oil from themselves, but it says that they were pouring "gold." The word oil placed in most Bibles in this passage of Scripture is in italics, meaning it is inferred by the translator. In the context of the rebuilding of the Temple, and the power emanating from the Holy Spirit, the Hebrew word picture is without rival. The anointing is as pure and valuable as gold. Light proceeds from the Giver of Life and permeates our Scriptures.

In the book of John, Jesus is recorded as walking in the area of Solomon's colonnade during the Feast of Dedication, or Hanukkah.

Then came the Feast of Dedication at Jerusalem. It was winter, and Jesus was in the temple area walking in Solomon's Colonnade. The Jews gathered around him, saying, "How long will you keep us in suspense? If you are the Messiah, tell us plainly."   John 10:22

Josephus, the historian of antiquity, left us important documentation. The story of Hanukkah is found in the Apocryphal book of Maccabees, one of the books in the collection of works preserved by the formal church. This holiday actually holds more historical resource in Christian literature than it does in the literature of the Jewish people. The holiday is not mentioned at all in the Old Testament because it happened after the writing of the book of Micah in the time period between the Testaments.

Hellenization of the World

The drama of Hanukkah begins with Alexander the Great. His conquest of the world at that time began in Greece in the fourth century, B.C. Alexander was so highly ambitious that he conquered the world by the age of 23. The book of the Prophet Daniel portrays him, symbolically, first as a leopard and later as a horned goat who charges so swiftly, that he does not even touch the ground. (Daniel 7:6, 8:5-7)

Thus, through the conquest of Alexander the Great, the hellenization of the world began. The ideas of Greek philosophers, glorifying the human body both in sport and in fine art, and the Greek way of perceiving the universe around us, permeated the world. These new philosophical ideas changed the existing cultures and sought to influence existing religions in conquered lands.

The Maccabean Revolt

Though our story of the Maccabean revolt against the Syrian-Greeks takes place much later, Alexander's conquest of the world is actually the foundation of those events. At his death, Alexander's empire split into four parts. The four generals of his vast army divided his conquests amongst themselves. Selucus, one of Alexander's generals, took what later became modern Syria. It was under the iron fist of this sector of the divided empire that Israel came to a time of great trouble.

Several generations from Selucus, a maniacal ruler came to power known as Antiochus Epiphanes. His name actually means "god in the flesh." Antiochus ruled from Syria but set up a military garrison in Jerusalem. This garrison was to oversee the hellenization of the population of Israel.

Antiochus had Jerusalem's high priest, Onais, murdered. He demanded that the circumcision of all Jewish baby boys cease. He had a statue of Jupiter erected on the Temple Mount and the sacrifice of swine on the altar was instituted.

The Syrian-Greek military garrison met their demise upon entering a small village outside Jerusalem called Modi'in. The soldiers built an altar and demanded a "show of allegiance" by having the local elders sacrifice a pig there. An old priest named Mattathias became so enraged when he saw what was taking place, that he killed the Jew who was complying with the orders. He and his sons fled to the nearby mountains to regroup and prepare to wage guerrilla warfare against the oppressive authorities of Syria.

Mattathias, being elderly, passed his leadership on to his son Judah, known as "the Maccabee" (meaning hammer), prior to his death. Judah, his brothers and their followers, the Hasmoneans, defeated every attempt by Antiochus to end his uprising. Their strategy and bravery could not be matched by the other side. In the face of astounding odds, Judah led his followers to Jerusalem where he drove the Syrian force from the Temple and out of the city.

Judah faced the grief of having to fight against his own Jewish brothers who had joined the side of the hellenizers. Some forsook their Jewishness for monetary gain, others for prestige. Some Israeli males even went so far as to surgically reverse their circumcisions in order to participate in nude Greek sporting events. They thereby erased any sign of their Jewish heritage, and the covenant in the flesh with the God of Israel.

On the twenty-fifth day of the Hebrew month Kislev, exactly the same day that three years earlier the Temple had been defiled by unholy sacrifices, the Hasmoneans liberated the city of Jerusalem and began in earnest to undo what their Syrian oppressors had done. They rushed to re-dedicate the desecrated Temple.

Temple Consecration

Arriving at the Temple site they began removing the stones of the defiled altar and toppling the statue of Jupiter. In the Holy Place inside the Temple stood the huge menorah. The rejoicing Jewish conquerors found earthenware oil cruses holding only enough oil to light the menorah for one day. The joy of the conquest of liberation was diminished due to the Levitical laws stating that the Temple menorah must burn "continually." It took eight days to process enough consecrated olive oil to replenish the menorah. How could they possibly begin the process and let the light go out again? Nevertheless, they lit the Temple menorah and began the process of procuring more oil.

A stamp of God's approval of their deeds of valor and zeal was evident when the oil which should have lasted for only one day, miraculously lasted the entire eight days until new oil was processed and consecrated. For this reason this 8-day holiday is also known as the "Festival of Lights."

Traditions

The traditions of the Feast of Hanukkah that have evolved over the years are the lighting of an eight-branched menorah (candle holder), called a *Hanukkiah*. One candle is lit each night by a candle known as the *shamash* or "servant" in English. Thus, the Hanukkiah candle holder has a total of nine candles. The candles are lit in a right hand to left hand order. Each night a new candle is added until the 8th day when all candles are ablaze with light. Hanukkah candles come in boxes of 44 since lighting one more each night of the eight nights including the shamash, adds up to 44.

The frying of potato pancakes in oil is traditional to commemorate the oil used to light the Temple Menorah for those eight days so long ago.

Games are played with a four sided top called a *dreidel*. Each side of the dreidel has a Hebrew letter on it standing for the slogan, *Nes Gadol Hiyah Po,* "A Great Miracle Happened Here." (Outside Israel, the Hebrew letters of the dreidel differ slightly, *Nes Gadol Hiyah Sham,* "A Great Miracle Happened There.")

Hanukkah Story Telling

The book of Maccabees is read, wherein lies the story of the bravery of those people zealous for God's ways. Women are expected to light the Hanukkiah candles during the holiday for two reasons. First, it is the woman who brings light and warmth to her home, and secondly, women played a role in this great drama as well. These accounts are retold concerning Israel's women of valor.

One story is about a woman named Judith, who upon seeing the desperate plight of her people, left Jerusalem and arrived at the Syrian encampment. Her beauty pleased the Syrian general and he, thinking to have her for himself, consented to her preparing him a meal. Judith knew that serving salted cheese would make the general thirsty, whereby she could overindulge him with drink. He complied, drinking wine, until he passed out. Judith seized the opportunity and cut off his head. When the Syrians learned of Judith's deed, and saw the Jews with their leaders head held aloft on a pole while advancing to attack, they fled.

Another story of a woman of valor relates that the Syrian governor passed a law that every Jewish bride would be brought to his own bed chamber first on the night of her wedding. The daughter of the high priest upon hearing this made plans for her own wedding ceremony. After her vows she stood amidst the people disrobing, almost like the prophet Jeremiah at a much earlier time. This, of course enraged the crowd. Her brothers shouted that they would kill her to which she replied, "Over my being disrobed you are angry, but about what the Syrian governor will do to me tonight you remain silent?" Being roused to righteous anger, her brothers stormed the palace and killed the Syrian governor and the revolt began.

What Does This Mean For Us?

This story is a tale repeated time and time again by the Jewish people. It is a story of overcoming in the face of overwhelming adversity. From the book of Genesis to the Maccabees the Jews have overcome Egyptians, the desert and its dangers, felled the walls of Jericho with rams horns, quelled the giants of the promised land, and led three Babylonian kings to the throne of God Almighty.

From the Maccabees to present day, there have been a string of miracles in Israel too long to list. But to answer Isaiah's rhetorical question, "Can a nation be born in a day?" Yes, indeed it can! In fact, it did happen, in the face of such overwhelming odds as to be absurd, should anyone simply have penned the story as a novel.

Our lesson from this holiday is that we can overcome with God. We will face Antiochus again in the visage of the Anti-Christ, but God's people will overcome. Satan's empire will once again be shattered. This time, God's people will watch because it will be done without hands, according to Daniel.

> *While you were watching, a rock was cut out, but not by human hands. It struck the statue on its feet of iron and clay and smashed them. Then the iron, the clay, the bronze, the silver and the gold were broken to pieces at the same time and became like chaff on a threshing floor in the summer. The wind swept them away without leaving a trace. But the rock that struck the statue became a huge mountain and filled the whole earth.*
>
> Dan. 2:34,35

From this, we can see that all oppression indeed will come to an end, so we can take courage. The message of the story of Hanukkah is that God is ever present in the annals of men and even greater, that His sovereign plan will be carried out without fail.

Hanukkah in Jerusalem

One of the best places to take a walk after dark during Hanukkah is the Jewish Quarter of the Old City of Jerusalem. The Quarter sits nestled inside walls rebuilt by Suliman the Magnificent, Sultan of the once powerful Turkish, Moslem, Ottoman Empire. He ruled here from 1517 AD until the British brought his kingdom to an end in 1917 AD.

Hanukkah candles are meant to be lit in a window facing outward to shed their light into the street. The beautiful architecture of the Jewish Quarter is the perfect environment. Narrow walkways between tall buildings made of creamy limestone seem to wait for candles to illuminate their soft façades. Long narrow passageways are warm and softly glowing. Bright spots punctuate the dark passageways bringing to mind the method Rembrandt used to illuminate the subjects in his paintings. Each succeeding day an extra candle graces the Hanukkah menorah shedding even more light.

The Jewish Quarter sits very high on a hill inside the confines of the walls of the Old City of Jerusalem. As one approaches the Temple Mount area, the topography drops off sharply into a valley. The view is spectacular both by day and by night.

My walk brought me to the edge of that valley to the staircase which leads down to the Western Wall plaza where the Jewish people pray today, There my daydream ended and I was brought back to reality. Riding the east wind coming from the Mount of Olives was the voice of the Moslem Muzzein declaring, "Allah is Great and Mohammed is his prophet." The contrast was almost too vivid.

Jerusalem is called the "City of Light" – it is the city where "the Light" walked and healed and illumined the dark eyes of some and the dark minds of those bound in spiritual darkness. Jerusalem is "ground zero" for future attempts of God's enemy to usurp His authority. The enemy works through people and the time is coming for confrontation between God's Kingdom of servants and Satan's kingdom of rebellion. Jerusalem will become more and more the focus of international attention. Jerusalem will never become politically acceptable for the western world. On the contrary, Jerusalem is appointed to become *"a cup of trembling for the nations,"* as Zechariah says. (Zech. 12:2)

But yet there is light. The symbolism of the eight-candle menorah being lit by a ninth "servant" candle, the shamash, is a reminder of the servanthood of the Messiah. Psalm 36:12 says, *"For with You is the fountain of life; in Your light we see light."*

We are, as God's servants, like the Hanukkah menorah. We are "servants" called to illuminate those around us and to ever increase the light. During Hanukkah, we see the candles being added daily until the glow almost drives back the chill of winter in the limestone city. Our calling, even though we know a deeper darkness is coming, is to continue to drive back the chill of winter with God's light.

If you have never considered Hanukkah as a holiday, I would encourage you to enjoy it. It is a definite encouragement to persevere in the face of crushing pressures. Hanukkah generally falls somewhere close to the Christian celebration of Christmas. My family keeps both, therefore, the following story of Christmas.

The Road To Bethlehem . . .
A Christmas Story

Since my family and I live in Israel, we have the wonderful privilege of visiting the birth place of our Messiah. Bethlehem lies not even 5 miles south of our home in Jerusalem and it has been our custom to go at least where we can see the city lit up on Christmas Eve. We sit and read the nativity story with Bethlehem's lights in the distance.

The time of year of Jesus birth is an interesting issue. Some think it to have been in the fall season, according to the courses of the priests who ministered in the Temple. Indeed, coupled with the priestly duties of Elizabeth's husband Zechariah, and the gestation period of Mary, this is probably true. The issue of whether or not we should celebrate Christmas at all is a question I have been challenged with in varying degrees both by Christians and by Jewish believers, and I feel it needs to be addressed briefly.

Throughout the Scriptures there are records of angelic visitations. In Luke chapter 2, we have a singularly notable event where a "great company of the heavenly host" appeared with the angelic messenger who came to proclaim the birth of the Messiah. There on the hills outside Bethlehem, they proclaimed the event which would split the earthly calendar. Their presence terrified the shepherds who had to be told "*fear not.*" Knowing that the heavenly host stood in a holy hush to punctuate this event, I am determined also to continue to celebrate His birth.

A few years ago, many of us here in Jerusalem were invited to form a choir and go to Bethlehem on Christmas Eve. Several hours of music in Praise of that wonderful event almost 2,000 years ago had been planned, rehearsed and polished for the event.

It was cold, "see your breath" weather. Rain had blown sideways for hours most of the afternoon of Christmas Eve. The choirs invited to sing knew the stage had been set up in the outside courtyard of the Church of the Nativity in Manger Square. Some were worried about being rained on. Some knew, God always prepares the path not only for the King, but also those desiring to minister to Him. Miraculously, it did not rain on us during the performance.

We live in the "real world" here in the Middle East. It is surprising to many visitors that it is not really the "Holy" Land as they would expect. It is a world of bus bombings and terrorist acts against civilians. Facing the facts on the ground, the Israeli government takes all precautions against potential terrorist attempts aimed at pilgrims. A half-way check point at Jerusalem's southern most bus station had been set up and all busses were to stop there for inspection before proceeding the few minutes on down the road to Bethlehem. All travelers knew that passports and other identification were a must.

In the cold rain we disembarked from the bus and stood in line to pass through the main building which had been set up efficiently as a check point. Those in line around me were grumbling about having to go though a checkpoint. In the mess of a cold rainy night in December in Jerusalem, I could understand the discomfort.

When the wait in line finally allowed me to pass through the doors of the building and view what was inside I had to choke back tears. Completely manned by Jewish people, helping Christians to make sure they had a memorable experience on Christmas Eve in Bethlehem, the building was a delightful, warmly decorated scene. Hot drinks and Christmas cake awaited each person coming through the line. Even the small gift of a single red rose was given to each person passing through.

I had to step to the side and gain control of myself. Men may cry in the '90s but they still don't like everyone to see it full face. Here were people whose parents had suffered persecution from "Christians" in Europe, Russia, and other countries. Some had not escaped. Instead they died in Hitler's ovens. In every age through Europe, there was persecution of the Jews, and many times on

Christian Holy Days. Here they were serving us, helping us, and wishing us a "Merry Christmas."

Even the road to Bethlehem, still in Jewish neighborhoods, was adorned with blocks of Christmas lights spelling out messages of warmth for the season.

All my defenses seemed to melt and I could not understand what I was seeing. I had to stand, tears in my eyes and apologize to God for the history that has made it so difficult to share our Hope with these people. People who, once you get to know, become friends forever. Then I had to go to each of those Jewish people on duty that rainy, cold Christmas Eve night and thank them for what they had done for us.

God took that opportunity to refresh in my mind exactly why He called my wife and I here to this postage-stamp-sized nation - to comfort His people, by living His Word and doing His deeds as His servants. It all boils down to - either being for the Jewish people or against them.

It became evident after living in Israel for awhile that it is all too easy to come here with our own agenda in mind and not keep our ears to the ground to see what it is that God is doing. It is easy to wind up running too fast to wait and hear what God is saying. Sometimes, when things do not go as we think they should, the desire to pack up and return to a former comfort zone is very real. God reminded me that the "comfort zone" exists in the words He gave us to say to His people.

> *Comfort, comfort My people, says your God. Speak tenderly to Jerusalem, and proclaim to her that her hard service has been completed, that her sin has been paid for, that she has received from the LORD's hand double for all her sins.*   Isaiah 40:1,2

Thankfully, there are many Christians who have also responded to this call of God and over the years have given their lives as volunteers here in the land. They are living testimony of the Messiah the Jewish people have never seen before. Truly, in this hour, many in the Church are choosing to pay the debt of love we have incurred over the centuries toward the Jewish people.

It is a side point but echoes my point in telling you this story. The Israeli government chooses to trim their forests in December in order to provide Christmas trees "free of charge" to the Christian community here in the land of Israel.

The situation in the last few years has changed dramatically. The Israeli government has had to turn Christmas festivities in Bethlehem over to the Palestine Authority since Bethlehem is now under their jurisdiction. Yassir Arafat, a Moslem in faith, now has full authority over the little town of Bethlehem. The words of the favorite Christmas song, "O Little Town of Bethlehem" no longer ring true. We can only pray that those Christians still living there will be spared the hate and rage of the new Moslem government which is opposed to Christians. From newspaper articles that have come to our attention, we know that some Christian Arabs left in this little town continue to endure terrible hardships.

This is not to purposefully relay to you a depressing Christmas story, but to point out that God is not finished with the Jewish people. Israel is the stage for the beginning and the end of the Bible epic.

The next Jewish holiday on the calendar falls in early Spring and centers itself around the book of Esther.

Purim

The "Lots" of Deliverance

The book of Esther unveils the ancient and captivating Persian world. Persian customs, and the splendor of the Persian empire are enthralling. The empire was far reaching in this time period. It encompassed nations such as Egypt, Babylon, Turkey and more. Much like stepping through Alice's Looking Glass, the book is a trip backward in time through a Persian, lattice-work window.

A plot so dramatic that it remains unrivaled for millennia, comes to life for us in the midst of the most colorful setting. In some scenes, one can almost smell desert jasmine in the air. Like gift wrapping, warm, still, summer nights with stars blazing above, and hot desert days enfold a story of God's compassion for His people.

So evident is the presence of God in the book of Esther, readers often find it hard to believe that, unlike other books of the Bible, the name of the God of Israel does not appear there once. God's intervention on behalf of His people is so obvious and all pervading that it borders on irony that His name does not appear on the pages of script.

The Jewish people have continued the celebration that was instituted when God led the enemies of His people to their own destruction. The celebration came to be known as *Purim*.

The word *Purim* is a Hebraization of the Aramaic word *pur*, meaning "lot." The Hebrew *"im"* ending simply makes the word plural. *Lots*, somewhat like drawing straws, were chosen in the book of Esther to determine the date upon which vengeance would fall upon the enemies of the Jewish people. These enemies had sought to destroy the Jews as a race. Purim is therefore, about deliverance.

Historical Purim

The Festival of Purim takes place on the 14th of the Jewish month of Adar, around February or March. The celebration is not a Levitical pilgrimage festival requiring the worshipper to come up to Jerusalem as is Passover (Pentecost), Shavuot (Feast of Weeks), and Sukkot (Feast of Tabernacles).

Purim is a microcosm of Jewish history. Here, like many other times in history, we find the Jews in exile and at the mercy of the whims of a local ruler. The handiwork of Heaven is constantly in view. Circumstances draw together in unusual ways that add up to more than just coincidence.

The awe-inspiring gardens of Persia, carved in stark contrast to the surrounding desert landscape, were the backdrop for a drama rivaling the best screen scripts of modern times. *Paradise*, by the way, is an ancient Persian word for "garden."

Ahasuerus, King Xerxes' Hebrew name, calls for Vashti his Queen to provide entertainment in the midst of a drunken banquet lasting 180 days. Refusing, she is dethroned and Esther, a young Jewish girl in exile from Jerusalem along with her people, is chosen to take her place. Esther's guardian, her cousin Mordecai, coaxes her as he stands on the sidelines, as this story unfolds.

Day after day, Mordechai refuses to pay homage to Xerxes' vizier, Haman, an Amelekite descendant. An incensed Haman, pleads with the king to destroy Mordechai and his people, the Jews. The king, unthinkingly, gives Haman authority to execute his plan.

Mordechai, hearing the plan, pleads with Esther to approach the king lest the Hebrews perish. Esther, with great planning and ceremony entertains the king for three days in Persian style. On a sleepless night, the king reviews the archival records and discovers that Mordechai had exposed a plot to murder the king.

Ahasuerus

Esther

Irony spices the plot as Haman is appointed to parade Mordechai through the streets arrayed in royal attire to honor him for his bravery. Haman's family prophecies his downfall from the event.

In a surprising plot reversal, Queen Esther exposes Haman for the evil creature he is in the presence of the king and all his court. In great anger, the king then has Haman hanged on the gallows he had constructed on which to hang Mordechai. In accordance with Persian law, all ten of Haman's sons are hanged along with him.

In ancient times, laws dictated that the sons of a felon were to be hanged along with him. In the scroll of Esther, the names of Haman's ten sons appear arranged as a verse of poetry. Tradition dictates that the reader of the scroll roll through the ten names in one breath as if to read through it with more than one breath might be a waste.

There is an interesting Hebrew word in Chapter 8, verse 17. God so thoroughly defended the Jewish population that great fear came on the rest of the population. The Hebrew verb "*Le'hityahadim*" (*mityahadim* is the verb form) which means to "*turn yourself into a Jew.*" The verse records that many of other nationalities became Jews because fear of the God of Israel was upon them.

This is not a suggestion for conversion. God has vital work for each one of us in the capacity in which we were born. Rather it stands as a testimony of the power of God to deliver His people against all odds, even in the face of potential annihilation as they cried out to Him with fasting, prayer, and desperation. In the book of Esther, where God's name is not even mentioned, He pervades every chapter and every character. Every twist of plot is orchestrated behind the scenes as if a puppet master were putting on a performance.

Mordechai

Purim Today

Purim has evolved into a holiday about rejoicing. Traditionally on Purim the book of Esther is read in the synagogue. Most Jewish congregations choose to read the story from an antique looking scroll called the *Megillat Esther*. For the sake of children, who can become bored if the reading goes on too long, an abbreviated version of the story is read.

The reading of the story is the focal point of Purim celebrations and actually acts as the starting gun for all the fun. During the reading of the story, when the name of Haman (the prime villain), is read, everyone in attendance is obliged to make as much noise as possible in order to fulfill the biblical injunction that Haman's name should be blotted out.

Haman

A wonderful tradition sets Purim aside from other holidays. Since Esther, being a young Jewish woman, rises to the exalted position of Queen in a nation wielding world power and is arrayed in royal finery, masquerading has become an enduring part of Purim. Her Uncle Mordechai, also is arrayed in royal finery and paraded through the streets of Shushan. Israeli children today act out this story by dressing up as Queen Esther, Mordechai, or even evil Haman and parading through the streets.

The party concludes with lots of music and good food, including the special triangle-shaped cookies called "Haman's Ears."

Conflict with Saddam

The theme, as I said before, is a microcosm of Jewish history. Saddam's past cat-and-mouse games with the United Nations Security Council has produced threats from just over Israel's eastern hills. Saber rattling and warnings crop up from time to time. Once before, in conflict with Saddam in 1991, the war began in January and miraculously ended exactly on Purim. An echo from an ancient story where God intervened for His people.

Purim may not be a Levitical feast, but the lesson is worth celebrating. God is able to deliver. Some of the other biblical feasts are also celebrations of God's mighty hand in awesome acts of deliverance. This celebration and other feasts of the Hebrew calendar remind us over and over again that we serve a God who is unswayed by the plots of the ungodly to oppose His people. We can read, celebrate, and be encouraged at God's great power and moreover, His great compassion and love.

Why We Remember

The stories of Hanukkah and Purim with their theme of plots against God's people bring to mind another period of history with a much darker tone - the Holocaust. Many people feel that history is history and now we should just forget. I believe that forgetting is tantamount to providing an opportunity for the repeat of history. I'd like to tell you why we should remember.

Carol, my wife, was privileged to be a backup singer for a popular Christian musician from Britain named Adrian Snell at *Yad Va'Shem* (the Holocaust Memorial Museum here in Jerusalem) for a concert. The Holocaust Museum has so appreciated Adrian's music over the years that they have had him perform there several times (somewhat surprising as he is a Gentile Christian). England's own BBC taped the concert the last time it was done at the museum. Adrian has dedicated much of his musical career to music that reflects the pain and loss of the Holocaust.

Adrian describes what he refers to as a "journey of questions" which began while he was working as a pop-star touring Europe, singing to soldiers at army bases in Germany. At one base in particular he said the concert was a major flop. The weather was wet, rainy, and muddy, and the atmosphere of the army base was extremely oppressive, so oppressive that he had serious trouble shaking off the dark foreboding feelings he was having.

Sharing his oppression with a soldier in the barracks where he was being housed, he received from him a knowing look along with an explanation that their barracks was only 3 miles from Bergen-Belsen, the former site of the extermination camp of Hitler's Third Reich. The base where he was being given hospitality with the soldiers had been used during World War II as an SS headquarters. The soldiers shared with him that they lived with the oppression on a daily basis. The darkness and oppression was not in Adrian's imagination.

Adrian took time to visit the nearby concentration camp. His trip to Bergen-Belsen planted questions in his mind that he has spent a lifetime finding answers to. Adrian is the son of an Anglican Bishop and was brought up in a loving Christian environment in the fear of the Lord.

During the concert, in this very special setting, I realized afresh that our job is to bring each other a little further on our journey. That journey is to fully understand the depth of the character of God and His incredible love for His people. One must be cautious about lightly answering questions regarding the Holocaust. Undoubtedly, it was the blackest time in the history of the world as we know it and trying to understand it leaves a crater in the human heart.

The concert was held in a section of Yad Va'Shem's Holocaust Memorial called the Valley of Lost Communities. It commemorates not just individuals, but the hundreds of entire Jewish communities that were exterminated in Europe by the Nazis. The Valley is man-made but awe-inspiring.

Canyons have been created by stacking rough hewn 4 foot by 4 foot square blocks of cream-colored limestone to the height of about 25 feet. Each stone is left ungroomed after being extracted from the quarry in the region of the upper Galilee. The extraction methods leave each stone with a distinct character of its own. The Valley is shaped like the map of Europe and is actually so big that you need a map to navigate through it without getting lost. It is more than impressive - it is monumental.

Chiseled in beautiful calligraphic lettering in the stone are the names of the areas of Europe where the Jewish communities once existed. Under each European area are chiseled the names of the communities themselves. As one wanders through the canyons the sky above seems just a slit of blue, looking as if it were a watercolor slash in a sea of beige limestone. The enormity of the monument echoes the enormity of the destruction. It is overwhelming.

Overwhelming but . . .

. . . This story must be told, again and again. The words of Elie Wiesel, a Holocaust survivor and now Israeli author and philosopher, were shared by Adrian as introduction to one of his songs called, "The Cry." The song's content is the murder of Abel by Cain. Abel's blood cries out to God from the ground and for the first time God experiences the absolute loneliness of murder.

"What have you done?" the song asks hauntingly and heavily. When God's anointing rests upon a musician, it provides a platform in which the Holy Spirit can reveal to you more of the character of God. During this song it was revealed to me that when one resists God's correction, whether you call it His wrath or only His discipline, only then does it become destructive. Cain was not utterly destroyed by God for his *act*. In fact he was marked by God for his own protection even in his exile. This theme of protection is also true of the children of Israel who were later taken away to Babylon. The book of Daniel is not about God's wrath or correction, - but rather, demonstrates His protection, promotion, and steering a nation filled with false gods toward the knowledge of the Holy One. We see God allowing opportunity for repentance. It is about places in time created by the Holy One in which mankind can assess their deeds. Elie Wiesel's words, paraphrased say . . .

". . . I am of a people and culture who view the murder of even one child as a blot upon mankind. I can not believe that one and a half million children were murdered by the Nazis. One must not think that any people can get away with that kind of act of evil. The end result should and would be the end of the world. None of us want that. Therefore, why do we remember? Why do we teach our children to remember such a black time in the history of mankind? Why are there places commemorating these events? It is, first of all, a method of restoring dignity to the people who died in such indignity and it is secondly a redemptive act. It is a way to bring to the forefront of mankind's thought processes these evil acts in order that repentance might take place.

"I see it as a way to postpone the destructive wrath of God against those responsible for the shedding of Abel's blood/Germany's Jews' blood."

This is why we remember. This is why the Bible's stories are recorded for us as well. We must remember - God commands us to remember His mighty acts of deliverance. That's why the Bible is filled with "rehearsal" times that we should remember the past to prepare for the future. Not just historical events but that we should consider ourselves, Jew or Gentile, as extended family with those Bible characters, sorrowing with them or rejoicing with them as if they were our own blood relations.

With this perspective from Elie Wiesel, the monumental beauty and proportions of the Valley of the Lost Communities was then filled with redeeming social value. It was more than the work of an artist in memory of lost loved ones. It was an active, living restoration of dignity. It was a redemptive act. It was a contact point for humanity to repent and embrace - and be embraced by God once again.

Stones are fundamental to the Jewish culture. Jacob's head rested on one as he dreamed of the gateway to heaven. The Israelites set them up as reminders of God's acts to and through mankind. The Children of Israel took them out of the river bed when crossing the Jordan River and created a monument of God's companionship in their wilderness journey just before they went into the Promised Land. The tribes set up a stone monument and called it *Ed* (meaning, "witness") to remind their descendants of their brotherhood with each other when two and a half tribes settled in what is now Jordan and southern Syria. Every Jewish person upon visiting a cemetery places a stone upon the grave marker instead of flowers. Jesus said that the stones would cry out if His disciples and the crowd did not proclaim His glory. He also stated that "*Upon this stone I will build My church*," likening Peter to a rock.

The massive stones of the Valley of the Lost Communities, each one different from the other, remind me now of thousands of generations of God's leading and love for His people. Therein is why we remember. Through this remembrance we bring dignity to the Holocaust, a grossly undignified and demonic act. We remember and teach our children to remember.

God's Faithfulness

This book is about remembering - God's way. We remember the good times, the times of Queen Esther and the victorious saga of the brave Maccabees. And though the good times are seasoned with the bad, we remember.

The new State of Israel was rebirthed in 1948 and stands as an ensign for His People, the Jewish People. They are coming home by the thousands just as the Bible predicted.

> *"However, the days are coming," declares the* LORD, *"when men will no longer say, 'As surely as the* LORD *lives, who brought the Israelites up out of Egypt,' but they will say, 'As surely as the Lord lives, who brought the Israelites up out of the land of the north, and out of all the countries where He had banished them.' For I will restore them to the land I gave their forefathers."*
>
> Jeremiah 16:14

They are returning and when they arrive, they are learning to observe the Feasts of the Lord, some for the first time in their lives. Some lived in repressive regimes where to this day they could not practice their faith. They are practicing for the heavenly events which those feast days foreshadow, remembering God's mighty acts of deliverance on their behalf and for the glory of His name.

Several years ago, my wife Carol and I joined a team of volunteers from Israel aboard the "Exodus Ship." On many successive trips the ship was responsible for transporting several thousand Russian Jewish people from the Ukranian Black Sea port of Odessa. We were privileged to be aboard one of the journeys representing Bridges for Peace, who had been asked to provide baby items for traveling mothers. Ukranian officials had been cruel to the Jewish women as they left the port on previous sailings by taking all their baby items from them. They left the mothers without baby bottles, formula, diapers, blankets, and other baby items. From Odessa to Haifa is almost a week's journey and mothers traveling without the necessities for a baby provided Bridges for Peace an opportunity to help.

On our sailing we were joined by a team of Israeli government officials who would transact immigration procedures enroute to Israel, plus we were accompanied by very large and official looking Israeli security men. Together we set sail from Haifa on what would be an exciting adventure.

The Bosphorus is a narrow channel that slices the Turkish city of Istanbul in half. Potential security hazards at this vulnerable point of the sailing meant security forces were a necessity aboard the ship. Our cargo was Jewish immigrants intent on living out a vision of making Israel their homeland. Sailing schedules and routes were kept secret to avoid acts of terrorism against the homecoming Jewish hopefuls.

Feasts of the LORD

We neared the Black Sea after several grueling days in a fierce Mediterranean winter storm. All aboard were seasick for three days until we came to the quiet waters of the Bosphorus. We watched as the amazing city of Istanbul slid by. High bridges hundreds of feet over our heads connected Asia and Europe. The Israeli security men stood outside on the deck of our ship watching carefully as we passed under the bridges around midnight. The minerets of the Hagia Sophia glided past. Once a glorious church edifice, it was turned into a mosque after the Moslem conquest. It seemed to want to tell its story, but Odessa called.

The crossing of the Black Sea was calm compared to the raging Mediterranean. We landed in Odessa and looked forward to loading on our precious cargo the next morning. When morning came I was stationed at the large cargo door of the ship at dock level. Pacing back and forth was a teenage Ukranian soldier. Snow was blowing lightly around the dock and the awe of being in a port of the former Soviet Union was overwhelming. I threw caution to the wind and stepped out of the ship, pointed my camera to take the young soldier's photo. The soldier froze - not from the snow but with the knowledge that I was about to take his picture. He screwed his face into the fiercest scowl he could manage and with a very clear gesture forbade me to click the shutter. He then motioned me back onto the ship. Like a whipped puppy I returned to work loading immigrant luggage into the hold. About an hour later, during a lull in the work, I heard a whistle from the dock. My soldier had arranged himself out of sight of his superiors and was striking a pose to have his picture taken. I laughed and obliged him. He was beaming.

Our job aboard the ship was to make the Russian families journey as easy as possible. We helped them find their rooms, carried luggage, even physically carried some aboard the ship who were too feeble to make it up the gangplank on their own. We organized games for the children to play and made many friends.

The return journey was incredible. Our journey to Odessa had been a nightmare of sea-sickness and lack of sleep from holding your body physically in your bed to keep from being thrown on the floor in the middle of the night. I didn't know a ship could move in so many directions. The return journey, however, was like a cruise ship. Snow gave way to sun. Cold turned to warm and the sea smiled. There was not so much as a ripple on the way back. We passed the Greek Islands like we were all on vacation. God was welcoming His people home in style.

One Russian Jewish man with whom we made friends told us how he had determined 12 years before to emigrate to Israel. At that time it was forbidden to emigrate out of the Soviet Union, but he did what he could anyway to prepare. He began to study Hebrew. Tears welled up in his eyes as he related his story. He now spoke Hebrew fluently. His dream was to travel to Israel on a ship. Now his dream had come true. He, his wife, and 14-year-old daughter, two grandparents, and sister were on board the ship coming home.

In the last few years our paths have crossed those of several of the people that were on that journey. They always have warm memories to relive. They remember that Carol was asked by the Israeli government officials to conduct a concert especially for the immigrants just before we landed at Haifa. They remember hearing the songs of Zion for the first time outside Russia and the anticipation that it built in their hearts, knowing they were within a few hours of stepping onto the soil of their homeland. The promise of centuries lay before them and they were going to live it.

We too will never forget. Prophecy is unfolding before our eyes and under our feet. God is faithful. His timing is not ours. I remember many years of demonstrating in front of Russian embassies in protest, and in front of Israeli government buildings in demonstrations of solidarity for the release of Russian refuseniks who had been imprisoned just for wanting to immigrate to Israel. Those were the days of the early '80s. Now here we are in a new phase of God's program. The lightening rod of Jewish resistance, Anatoly Shcharansky who spent 14 years in Soviet prisons, three of them in solitary confinement, is now a member of the Israeli Parliament. Arrested minutes after his wedding to Avital, Anatoly now is actively involved with the issues of governing his home State, Israel.

It is truly wonderful to be a part of fulfillment of prophecy.

I hope you have been inspired to look at the Feasts of the Lord in a new light. Maybe you have looked at them for the first time. I know you will find the joy in researching them and celebrating some of them as my family has done. They are like a string of pearls. They grace the year with seasons of reflection on God's appointed times. Indeed they are times of rehearsal for the end of time.

Passover	Shavuot	Rosh Hashana	Days of Awe	Yom Kippur
Redemption	Revelation & the Holy Spirit	Obedience Provision	Repentance & Restitution	Covering & Forgiveness

Simchat Torah	Hanukkah	Purim
Rejoicing & Thanksgiving	Light & Zeal for God's Ways	God's Deliverance

May God bless you richly   –   keep your ears open for the sounding of the Great Shofar!

About the Author

Ron Cantrell is Publication Manager for Bridges for Peace, an evangelical Christian ministry located in Jerusalem, Israel, whose aim is to build understanding between Christians and Jews, both in Israel and worldwide. He is a member of King of Kings Assembly in Jerusalem and leads a weekly Bible study.

Ron has been involved in Christian ministry for the past 31 years as a pastor, Bible school teacher, and photojournalist. He has taught Old Testament Bible Survey, Public Speaking, Photography, and Journalism at the Christians In Action Bible school in Southern California before moving with his family to Israel in the 1980s. These job descriptions have all come together in an effort to bring to Christians a deeper understanding of the nation of Israel and the Jewish community worldwide.

Ron and his wife, Carol, desire that believers would reap the benefit of that richness with the discovery of the living roots of Christianity in its Hebraic setting. We are enriched as we view the books of the Bible from the perspective of the culture in which they were written.

Ron, Carol and two of their three children are presently living and ministering in Jerusalem, Israel, where they have lived for over 14 years.

For personal correspondence or speaking itinerary:

Ron Cantrell
P.O. Box 7304
Jerusalem, Israel
Fax: 972-2-566-6675
E-mail: ron715@netvision.net.il

For current news, and information of issues regarding Israel visit the Bridges for Peace website at: www.bridgesforpeace.com

Bibliography

De Koven, Rabbi Ralph. *A Prayer Book with Explanatory Notes.*
KTAV Publishing House Inc., 1965.

The Encyclopedia Judaica, Keter Publishing House, Ltd.
Jerusalem, Israel 1978

Fleming, Dr. Jim. *Jesus in the Biblical Feasts*, Biblical Resources, Jerusalem, Israel

Herodotus, *Histories.* Wordsworth Classics of World Literature,
Wordsworth editions limited. Cumberland House, 1996

Jacq, Christian. *Ramses: The Son of Light Vol. I*, Time Warner Books, 1995.

Jordan, Michael. *Encyclopedia of Gods*, Kyle Cathie Limited; first printing 1922;
copyright 1992 Michael Jordan.

Siegal, Richard; Strassfeld, Michael; Strassfeld, Sharon. *The First Jewish Catalog.*
The Jewish Publication Society of America, 1973.

Strassfeld, Michael. *The Jewish Holidays: A Guide and Commentary,*
Harper & Row, Publishers, New York, 1985.

Yamauchi, Edwin M. *Persia and the Bible*, Baker Books,
first paperback edition, 1996.